ENDORSEMENTS

"Many believers today long for a return to the faith practices of our spiritual ancestors. These pilgrims rank "tested" over "trendy," "time-worn" over "hip," and "liturgical" over "entertaining." In this, her concise guide through the ancient paths, *Thrive: Life-Giving Disciplines for a Chaotic World,* spiritual director Markene Meyer gently re-introduces sojourners to the ways our elders knew. Highly recommended."

Sandra Glahn, seminary professor and author of the
Coffee Cup Bible Study series

"In our fast-paced society that is increasingly hostile to Christianity, how can the believer consistently notice and thrive in Christ's presence? In *Thrive,* Markene Meyer beautifully describes ancient, timeless spiritual disciplines and walks the believer through life-giving practices that can help us live free from the tyranny of modern culture."

Penna Dexter, Co-host, Point of View Radio Show

"I strongly endorse *Thrive: Life-Giving Disciplines for a Chaotic World* by Markene Meyer. In this innovative work, Meyer suggests adopting a rule of life, which can help govern our busy habits in these high-tech times. The applications are based upon practices deeply rooted in church history. This book should be read with a cup of coffee in one hand . . . and a highlighter in the other. The penetrating questions truly made me think and forced me to examine my own patterns and natural reflexes. I want to live in a *life-giving* way and I know Meyer's scholarship will help me see the path."

Dr. Paul Pettit, Professor of Pastoral Ministries,
Dallas Theological Seminary

D1260573

"I always like a book that makes me think. But I love a book that invites me on a personal journey of discovery and spiritual growth. *Thrive: Life-Giving Disciplines for a Chaotic World* is such a book. Markene Meyer deftly crafts an experience that encourages readers to engage in spiritual practices that have stood the test of time while considering how their culture affects their current lifestyle. Throughout the exercises and group encounters, participants are led to thoughtfully consider and embrace those activities which enliven their relationship with God and nurture a life of love."

— Debbie Swindoll, Executive Director of Grafted Life Ministries

"*Thrive: Life-Giving Disciplines for a Chaotic World* is a very useful introduction to the profound wisdom of the ancient *Rule of St. Benedict*. Markene Meyer's work is accessible and directed toward practice. She provides insight and instruction for the reader who is moving along this time-tested way of Christian formation—practices and rhythms that encourage our inward conformity to the likeness of Christ and the enjoyment that comes with our relationship with God and neighbor. This is a welcomed help in a time such as ours."

— The Rev. Aaron J. Jeffrey, Lecturer in Theology, Culture and Christian Formation, and Director of Anglican Studies and Ministerial Formation, Redeemer Theological Seminary

"In *Thrive: Life-Giving Disciplines for a Chaotic World*, Markene Meyer brings practical clarity to our understanding of Spiritual Disciplines and provides meaningful ways in which the Spiritual Disciplines can be employed today to facilitate our growth in Christ. Practices we have dismissively relegated to the past become both relevant and effective in the spiritual development we long for in the midst of the tremors of today's unstable world. Through the years the evangelical community has been rightly focused on the Word of God. *Thrive* gives us a practical means to see Scripture impact and enrich our lives even more deeply."

— Andrew Seidel, Adjunct Professor, Dallas Theological Seminary

"*Thrive* is a guide book for spiritual travelers who are worn out, worn down, and in search of a path - a way - that is trustworthy and life-giving. In our age of novelty and disposability and consequently consumerism and infidelity, Markene Meyer guides us to the well-worn path of St. Benedict and shows us how we can walk the ancient paths to wholeness and holiness in the 21st century. Philosopher Alastair MacIntyre has said we are currently in need of 'another—doubtlessly very different—St. Benedict.' Many people have bantered about what this new Benedict Option might look like, and here Meyer has given us an excellent proposal."

The Rev. Canon David Roseberry, Provincial Canon for Mission, ACNA

THRIVE

LIFE-GIVING DISCIPLINES FOR
A CHAOTIC WORLD

MARKENE MEYER

AUTHENTICITY
BOOK HOUSE

Authenticity Book House
c/o Proven Way Ministries
The Hope Center
2001 W. Plano Parkway, Suite 3422
Plano, TX 75075

Thrive: Life-Giving Disciplines for a Chaotic World
Copyright © 2016 by Markene Meyer
ISBN: 978-1-943994-68-3

All rights reserved. No part of this book may be used or reproduced by any means, graphic, electronic, or mechanical, including photocopying, recording, taping or by any information storage retrieval system without the written permission of the publisher except in the case of brief quotations embodied in critical articles and reviews.

All scripture quotations, unless otherwise indicated, are taken from the New *American Standard Bible*, copyright © 1960, 1962, 1963, 1968, 1971, 1972, 1973, 1975, 1977 and 1995 by the Lockman Foundation. Used by permission.

Scripture quotations marked "KJV" are taken from the Holy Bible, King James Version, Cambridge, 1769.

Scripture quotations marked "The Message" are taken from *The Message*. Copyright © 1993, 1994, 1995, 1996, 2000, 2001, 2002. Used by permission of NavPress Publishing Group.

Because of the dynamic nature of the Internet, any web addresses or links contained in this book may have changed since publication and may no longer be valid.

Published by Authenticity Book House
Cover designed by A. J. Geiger
Interior design & Typesetting by Ramesh Kumar Pitchai

Printed in the United States of America

10 9 8 7 6 5 4 3 2 1

AUTHENTICITY
BOOK HOUSE

TABLE OF CONTENTS

To those faithful Christ-followers whose authentic love and joy attracted me to a life in which I could truly thrive.

PREFACE

Ask for the ancient paths, where the good way is, and walk in it; and you will find rest for your souls.

JEREMIAH 6:16

For years my family has traveled through the Texas Panhandle on our way to the Colorado Rockies. We know the route well, where we can find authentic Texas barbeque, stop-worthy produce stands, or roadside attractions like Cadillac Ranch. Although there are a few changes year to year, we thought we knew every bend in the road—from notorious small-town speed traps to where the mountains first come into view. Despite the familiarity of these roads, one spring we took a wrong turn and found ourselves in the tiny town of Stratford, ten miles south of the Oklahoma state line. As we coasted into town, one of our tires blew out, so we pulled into the mechanic for a patch. While we waited we browsed the local hardware store. We stocked up on heavy socks and smiled at the cacophony of chirping chicks huddled under warming lamps. The truth was, after navigating these roads for decades we didn't think we needed a map. But that trip became a kind of spiritual metaphor for me, a reminder that no matter how familiar the way seems, it's beneficial to consult a road map.

Whether by design or default, we each approach life in a particular way. Some of us plan and prepare, mapping things out like compulsive boy scouts trying to anticipate every contingency, while others of us give little thought to the way in which we live. We're careening down the roadway of life without a map. For many of us, if we pause long enough to get our bearings, life feels more chaotic than intentional, more frustrating than fulfilling, more exhausting than life-giving, or a crazy quilt of all of the above. Upon examination, each of our lives reveals a unique patchwork of rhythms, practices, and relationships, a reflection of countless choices made each day. Yet how thoughtful are we about living in a way that truly reflects our desires and intentions as Christ-followers? For that matter, are we living in a way that's sustainable, continually renewed and restored by God's Spirit, or are we barely hanging on until the next weekend getaway?

Our Lord invites us to follow his way. The way that leads to life (Matt. 7:13–14). Jesus has gone before us, and Jesus accompanies us on our journey. Jesus invites us into a relationship, not a belief system or set of practices. Certainly we follow his beliefs and practices, but the journey of the Christian life is about life-giving relationship. About knowing and being known. Knowing our God, the One who knows, loves, and cherishes us. Knowing and being known by others with whom we share the living Spirit of Jesus Christ. Over time, these abiding relationships form, shape, and profoundly change us. In Christ, and in authentic community with others in Christ, we flourish and find new life. Jesus came to bring us life—the joy-filled, faith-inspired, self-giving kind of life he lived.

Jesus gave his life that we might live our life in relationship with him—following his ways and relying on his abundant presence and power. "Lord Jesus Christ, you stretched out your arms of love on the hard wood of the cross that everyone might come within the reach of your saving embrace."[1] Jesus gave his life that we might receive new life and live in a way that brings life to us and to those around us. Jesus offers a way which he enables by his indwelling Spirit. As we follow Christ each day, depending on him for life and godliness (2 Pet. 1:3), he renews and sustains our soul.

"Come to Me, all who are weary and heavy-laden, and I will give you rest" (Matt. 11:28). Jesus welcomes those of us who are worn out by doing things our way—a way, if we are honest with ourselves, that doesn't work. A way that sometimes leaves us in the middle of nowhere with a flat tire and a cart full of socks we don't need. Jesus sees our soul weariness and offers us a different way.

In very practical terms, what does it look like to follow Jesus Christ in the 21st century? In the chapters before us, we'll consult some ancient roadmaps in order to discern a more life-giving way for today. Although few of us are likely headed for a cloistered existence, the monastic *Rule of St. Benedict* (6th c.) will serve as our inspiration. We'll examine classic monastic themes such as fidelity, attentiveness, rhythm, self-giving, renunciation, and love for the world. We'll practice time-tested spiritual disciplines such as scripture meditation, silence and solitude, *examen*, and fixed-hour prayer. Along the way we'll consider our own way of life: values and priorities, gifts and abilities, dreams and longings, our relationship with Christ and one another. We'll consider the implications of this ancient way of life for our life of faith today, culminating in writing a rule of life—a simple guideline for living that expresses our desires and intentions as Christ-followers.

The term "rule" comes from the Latin word *regula,* which is at the root of the English word "regular." It carries with it the ideas of rhythm, regularity, and repetition. A rule of life offers a pattern or guide by which monastic communities or other gathered believers live out of devotion to Christ. Like the Benedictine monks, who structure their lives around a daily rhythm of prayer and work, we can emphasize certain rhythms, practices, and relationships out of love for Christ and desire to grow in likeness to him. A rule of life is not a rigid list of do's and don'ts. Rather, a rule of life is a gentle guideline that helps us order our life around relationship with Jesus Christ, to live in a way in which we truly thrive.

Using this Book with a Small Group

I've tailored the material in this book to a small-group format and written each chapter, associated questions, and spiritual discipline with a weekly group conversation in mind. I encourage you to read this book in the company of several spiritual friends for mutual encouragement, prayer support, and accountability. As the Benedictine monks pledged to support each other in fidelity to Christ, I pray you will uphold one another in your mutual pursuit of a way of life which brings life and honors God. I encourage you to read the meeting guidelines in the Thrive Group Leader Guide, Appendix F.

As you will see, each chapter reveals an aspect of monastic life which helps us draw near to Christ. We'll explore the ways in which these classic ideals and practices find expression in the scriptures, the historic church, and the monastic way of life. We'll consider these ideals and practices in light of the broader culture in which we live. At the end of each chapter I've provided a few questions for reflection and discussion of the chapter theme and a related aspect of your own way of life. As you journey through *Thrive*, I encourage you to regularly consider three questions: How is it with your soul (see chapter 3)? Where are you noticing God lately? And, how is God inviting you to respond to what you are noticing? Reflecting on these kinds of questions with some consistency can foster awareness of Christ's presence and how Christ is inviting us to respond to his presence.

Finally, following each chapter I've included instructions for practicing a spiritual discipline related to the chapter theme. As you explore these time-honored disciplines, I pray the Lord will help you discern rhythms, practices, and relationships which help you draw near to him. For the final spiritual discipline, you'll pull together the work you've done in each chapter and write a simple rule of life for the near term—the next season, semester or few months. May you truly thrive as you discover ways to connect more deeply each day with Christ, "the way, the truth, and the life" (John 14:6).

Notes

1. *The Book of Common Prayer* (New York: Church Publishing Incorporated, 1979), 101.

CHAPTER 1

Benedict of Nursia: An Unlikely Guide for the Journey

Part one of the monk's fantasy is the decision not to live as everyone else does. The man or woman looks around and sees a way of life that is chaotic, irreverent, or unethical and decides to design a life according to different standards. Part two is sketching out the new way in a rule. . . . From the creative point of view, the monastic rule is an instrument for shaping a particular kind of life for which a person has a deep and genuine desire.

THOMAS MOORE

For guidance on our journey we turn to an unlikely source, a humble young man born in northern Italy about five hundred years after Jesus walked this earth. It was a time of great geo-political and socio-economic change. The power structures of the Roman Empire were crumbling. Waves of barbarian invasions, plague, and economic hardship brought instability and chaos to the region. Following the custom of that time, young Benedict leaves his family in Nursia to pursue his education in Rome. Discouraged by the abject immorality around him, he renounces the world to live a solitary life of holiness. But his solitary existence is short-lived, for he gains a reputation as a wise and virtuous man. People increasingly seek his counsel, and he eventually founds a dozen or so monasteries, the largest, Monte Cassino, which he oversees as their abbot.

In about 530 AD, Benedict composes a *regula* or rule of life for the community gathered around him at Monte Cassino. Benedict wrote his *regula* or the *Rule of St. Benedict* as a pastoral guide for the devout follower of Christ—a compilation of ideals, guidelines, and practices for people desiring to grow in virtue and likeness to Christ. Benedict's unassuming rule sparks a movement, and he becomes known as the father of Western monasticism. For over 1500 years the *Rule of St. Benedict* has been an enduring spiritual guide for many. We can sum up his philosophy in a simple exhortation. "Your way of acting should be different from the world's way; the love of Christ must come before all else" (*RB* 4).[1]

Benedict urges his followers toward a way of life that looks markedly different from the world, one characterized by sacrificial love for Christ and others, one lived within a loving community of like-minded individuals pursuing the common objective of imitating Christ. Benedict urges his followers to the kind of life Christ lived. "Jesus said to His disciples, 'If anyone wishes to come after Me, he must deny himself, and take up his cross and follow Me'" (Matt. 16:24). Benedictine monks live out this self-giving way of life in service to their community and the world around them.

The *Rule of St. Benedict* is a fairly brief rule, about seventy-three chapters in length. The Prologue and first seven chapters provide a kind of philosophical or doctrinal foundation, including chapters on each of three key virtues—obedience, restraint of speech, and humility. The remaining chapters concern practical matters such as prayer and worship practices, procedures for addressing "faults" or shortcomings (always for the sake of reform), and instructions for aspects of the common life such as sharing of goods or offering hospitality to guests. In the Epilogue we learn that Benedict wrote his little rule so that in observing it we can "show some degree of virtue and the beginnings of monastic life" (*RB* 73). For "observant and obedient" monks, monastic rules offer "tools for the cultivation of virtues" (*RB* 73). Both in Benedict's day and in ours, we might choose to abide by a simple rule of life out of a desire to draw near to Christ and grow in virtue and likeness to him.

We often view the *Rule of St. Benedict* through a thick cultural lens. But in examining monastic rules in existence during Benedict's time (such as the overbearing *Rule of the Master*, author unknown), Benedict's *Rule* tends toward moderation and common sense. He urges that all be done with wisdom, discretion, love, and concern for the well-being of the community. This is perhaps one of the reasons his rule endures when other monastic rules have fallen by the wayside. In the Prologue, Benedict informs us, "We intend to establish a school for the Lord's service. In drawing up its regulations, we hope to set down nothing harsh, nothing burdensome. The good of all concerned, however, may prompt us to a little strictness in order to amend faults and to safeguard love" (*RB* Prologue).

Corporate Rhythms and Practices

Communal rhythms or shared patterns of practice lend life-giving structure to monastic community. Three essential components make up Benedictine daily life—prayer, scripture meditation, and work. The "divine office," their liturgy or communal prayers, provides an ordering rhythm. Eight times each day, the monks gather for prayer. *Every other activity orders around the predominant rhythm of daily prayer.* Personal scripture study or meditation (*lectio divina*) serves as a second and closely related activity. Manual labor or work comprises the third aspect of daily life. Members assume various responsibilities that serve and sustain the monastic community, and often, the communities around them. In one way or another, each of these three components finds expression in a typical day. Daily the community invests about three hours in corporate prayer, two or three hours studying the scriptures, and five hours in some kind of manual labor.[2] Day after day. Year after year.

In compiling his *Rule* Benedict relies heavily on the Bible, including more than 300 direct quotations or scripture references.[3] He upholds scripture as the best rule, the best guideline for living. Benedict's little book serves as a mere supplement to the Bible. "What page, what passage of the inspired books of the Old and New Testaments is not the truest of guides for human life" (*RB* 73)? Not only does scriptural truth shape the philosophy of the *Rule*, the words of the scriptures fill the monks' daily practices. Each day the community participates in scripture-rich practices such as prayer, worship, meditation, or study, as well as recitation and singing during work. The monks eat their meals in silence while someone reads from the scriptures or other devotional writing. It may be experienced in various ways, but scripture saturates Benedictine life.

From the *Rule of St. Benedict* we gain insight into the ideals and practices of the devout men and women who live in these communities. For our purposes here, we're not as concerned with the letter (or specific practices) of these monastic rules, but more the spirit contained within them. Indeed, some practices may seem a bit harsh to our modern sensibilities. But as we will see, the rhythms, practices, and relationships of Benedictine life are all intended to foster awareness and response to Christ.

In the chapters ahead, we'll explore this way of life in more depth, considering the implications for a life of faith today. At its simplest, life in monastic community is about noticing Christ's presence in and around us, in all of life, and following closely after him. The *Rule of St. Benedict* invites us to pay attention to Christ's presence and to the way we live in response to his presence. As you will see, a rule of life is not about keeping rules, it's about keeping relationship. In the chapters ahead, I invite you to follow the way of the ancients and pen your own rule of life, a gentle guideline for ordering your life around a life-giving relationship with Jesus Christ.

The Influence of the Broader Culture

As explained in the Preface, in each chapter we'll explore these ancient Christian ideals in light of the contemporary cultural context in which we live. We'll compare and contrast each monastic theme with perspectives and practices we find in the predominant culture today. Before we begin our discussion, let's define some terms. First, I'm defining culture as the expression of what a particular group values. These values often find expression in three areas. Specifically, the practices (what a group does), convictions (what a group believes), and narratives (the stories that a group tells) articulate the unique story of each particular culture.[4]

When discussing culture, let's keep a few things in mind. First, culture is not singular. We each function within multiple subcultures. We're each born into a unique family of particular origin and ethnicity. We live in a specific community and region within a particular country. We work in a specific vocational context, and we express our faith and other interests in various overlapping communities. Practices, convictions, and narratives vary among subcultures.

Second, culture doesn't exist "out there." Sometimes trying to understand our cultural context feels like asking a fish to describe the water in which it swims. We're so immersed in our culture (and subcultures) that we find ourselves too close to see it clearly. That's one of many reasons why travel to other cultures can prove valuable. In experiencing practices, convictions, and narratives different from our own, we gain fresh perspective on our own culture.

Third, culture isn't inherently evil, but an expression of collective values as seen in a culture's practices, convictions, and narratives. At the same time, culture isn't neutral. The practices, convictions, and narratives that make up a culture give it a particular shape and influence. Finally, we're not merely influenced by culture, we influence it as well. Through the choices we make every day, we contribute to the form and shape of the culture in which we live.

The broader culture can greatly influence us, but perhaps in ways we've never considered. As followers of Christ desiring to grow in his likeness, we ought to pay attention to the ways our wider cultural context tends to form us. Author Philip Kenneson explains, "I believe that our call to be 'salt' and 'light' in the world requires us to understand the dominant cultural forces that are shaping both the church and the world around it. . . . There is much about the dominant culture that makes it difficult for anyone to nurture a life of virtue."5 In other words, thoughtful observation of the culture around us can enlighten both our personal witness and pursuit of Christlikeness. In Kenneson's opinion, the broader culture in which we live does not tend to incline us toward Christian virtue.

We'll paint in broad strokes here, but allow me to pose a question worth considering: Generally speaking, into what or whom might the current prevailing culture tend to form us? Consumers? Cynics? Narcissists? Kenneson addresses this subject in *Life on the Vine*, contrasting the ways God forms us in likeness to Christ (illustrated by the nine virtues or fruit of the Spirit, Gal. 5:22–23), with the ways the predominant culture tends to form us. He encourages us to examine our cultural practices more carefully, cautioning, "Too often we are pledging allegiance to Christ with our lips while engaging in practices that cultivate a quite different set of loyalties, dispositions, and convictions."6

In other words, over time the habitual choices, practices, and patterns of our daily lives contribute to the form and shape of our character. And some practices promoted by the broader culture nurture "loyalties, dispositions, and convictions" that run counter to our faith. Some cultural practices may form us in ways contrary to the way in which God desires to form us. Kenneson advises, "As Christians, we have a long way to go in learning to identify and resist the full range of cultural practices that inhibit a life of the Spirit."7

One way of participating in our own growth and formation, one way of thriving in relationship with Christ, is by abstaining from practices that might inhibit the transformational work of God's Spirit in us. As Christ-followers we would do well to consider which cultural practices might actually hinder our growth in likeness to Christ. To take it a step further, Kenneson suggests we may need *alternative* practices, "that can both *curb* the dominant culture's power over our lives and *nourish* a way of life capable of producing the fruit of the Spirit" (emphasis added).8 Essentially, I'm suggesting we need to approach our way of life more thoughtfully. I'm asking us to consider in what ways we might find ourselves influenced by the practices, convictions, and narratives of the broader culture.

In your weekly Thrive Group conversation, I encourage you to discuss some of these cultural influences from several perspectives. First, you'll want to consider how certain cultural influences potentially *inhibit* life in the Spirit. In the culture in which you live, which particular practices could hinder your growth in likeness to Christ? On the flip side you'll want to identify some personal practices which help you attend more thoughtfully to your relationship with Christ. Which daily practices might *nurture and deepen* your relationship with Christ?

Finally, in very practical terms, how will your observations of culture shape your rule of life? For example, in relation to the consumerism prevalent in Western culture, you may want to reflect on your orientation toward material things. What did Christ teach about the place of material things in our lives? What priority do you desire for material things to have in your life? What might this look like in your rule of life?

Of course, living differently from the predominant culture can bring real challenges. But Christ invites us to a different way of life. Christ invites us to a way enabled by his presence, full of his joy, revealing the virtues, values and priorities of his gracious kingdom. Though we remain in the world, Christ calls us out of the world. And our lives will reflect this. We write and live by a rule of life to articulate the ways our life will differ from the world around us. Thomas Moore, who lived as an Augustinian monk for twelve years, agrees, "It's a tough life in certain ways—the rule can be harsh—but it is also in its own way liberating. It frees a person from the unspoken rules of the society at large and offers an alternative."9

A More Life-Giving Way

As we begin to look at writing a rule of life, I invite you to reflect on several preliminaries. This week, you'll want to examine your current way of life and begin discerning which aspects are life-giving for you. How do I define life-giving? Anything that draws us near to Christ brings us life. Like the Benedictine monks, as Christ-followers we share certain soul-nourishing practices such as prayer, worship, or scripture meditation. We'll explore some of these classic spiritual disciplines in the pages ahead. As you read through this guidebook, a first step toward a more life-giving way is to *notice* those particular rhythms, practices, and relationships which help you draw near to Christ.

The God that made and cherishes us is present each moment of our days, continually speaking into our lives and drawing us into relationship with him. Christ draws us to himself in innumerable ways. For example, perhaps you're drawn to Christ while enjoying the natural world, creation in all its beauty and wonder. Pay attention to this as you write a simple rule. Build a few moments outdoors into each day, a walk, a moment of prayer, some time in your garden. Or perhaps you delight in God while enjoying beauty, whether beautiful music, art, or architecture. You might find fellowship with God while enjoying the magnificence of a classical masterpiece like Vivaldi's *Four Seasons* or Handel's *Water Music*. Perhaps you can build some concert events or art museum visits into your monthly rhythms.

Or perhaps you tend to notice God while creating art, working with your hands in some way, or enjoying some kind of physical activity like a bike ride. In his brief treatise, *Practicing the Presence of God*, 17th century Carmelite monk Brother Lawrence reminds us that even in the most ordinary moments of life, whether washing dishes or peeling potatoes, we can find the sweetest communion with God. All of our lives include the ordinary. Seize on these moments as opportunities for silent prayer and attentiveness to God's presence.

Sometimes we discover God's nearness as we serve others in the humblest of ways, caring for a child, a neighbor, or aging parent. Many of us find consolation in the company of fellow Christ-followers. We need each other. Pay attention to those relationships which are life-giving for you and nurture them. And look for opportunities to speak life into other people's lives. Begin to think about how you can build these kinds of soul-nourishing elements into your life rhythms.

God speaks to us in countless ways. I've only mentioned a few here. I invite you to begin discerning those rhythms, practices, and relationships which draw you near to him in the day to day of life. I invite you to consider what kind of life Christ is inviting you to live.

Second, in considering your current way of life, which aspects do not necessarily bring life? Are there particular aspects of life you find difficult, challenging, or taxing? Why do you think this is? Have you invited God into these areas of life? As you look at the current rhythms, practices, and relationships of your life, which aspects reflect the way you desire to live as a follower of Christ and which do not? Begin to consider what changes you might make going forward.

Finally, as I've noted, Benedictine community draws strength and nourishment from the scriptures in many aspects of daily life. Make note of any scriptures which could offer foundation or direction in your life. What makes these scriptures personally significant and in what ways might they inform and shape your rule or way of life?

I know, I'm asking big questions here. At this point you may or may not have many answers. That's okay. Highlight or underline the questions in each chapter and come back to them when you're ready. Keep in mind that discerning a life-giving way, your own "rule of life," is a lifelong process. I'm only asking you to consider the short-term here, the next season or semester, but I encourage you to revise your rule of life several times a year as circumstances change. Some elements will carry over from year to year. Others will shift as the Spirit leads.

Christ will accompany you on this journey of discovery, walking with you every step of the way. As you seek to discern a way of life, he will guide you. I invite you to approach each question in this book prayerfully and trust God with the answers. May you sense Christ's nearness and may he bless your desire to find a more life-giving way. May God bless your efforts to discern your own "alternative" way of living as a follower of Jesus Christ.

Questions for Reflection and Discussion[10]

1. **Reflect on the Word**

   Scriptures such as Matthew 22:34–40 or John 5:19 provide examples of a kind of "rule" or way of life typical of our Lord. What does each passage indicate about the rhythms, practices, and relationships in Christ's life? Which other scriptures give insight into his way of life?

2. **Reflect on our world**

   List some of the practices, convictions, and narratives that characterize your broader contemporary culture. How might these compare and contrast with the practices, convictions, and narratives upheld by Christ or his followers?

   How might the four observations of culture (culture is not singular; culture is not "out there"; culture is not inherently evil, and culture is not neutral) influence the way you engage with your own culture?

3. **Reflect on your spiritual journey**

   Although you may never have written a rule of life before, everyone lives in a particular way. Take time to notice the rhythms, practices, and relationships of your life. What are they? Which aspects are life-giving for you? Which are not? What kinds of rhythms, practices, and relationships are more life-giving for you? What kinds of changes would you like to make going forward?

4. **Reflect on your rule of life**

   Which particular scripture passages might form the foundation of your rule of life? Why are these significant for you?

   In the near term (next season, semester or few months), what ways could you regularly engage with God's Word in a meaningful way?

   Examples:
   1) This fall I'll invite several neighbors to my home for an informal study of Philippians.
   2) In the morning I'll read the daily scripture readings in the Daily Office Lectionary in the *Book of Common Prayer* (or other devotional or online scripture reading plan).

5. **This week, read the Introduction to Spiritual Disciplines and complete Spiritual Discipline 1: Scripture Meditation (following).**

Introduction to Spiritual Disciplines

Grace is God's sustaining and transforming power. The grace of God that has reconciled us and saved us is . . . also his marvelous power that is able to remake us into new people.

JAMES WILHOIT

God has given us the disciplines of the spiritual life as a means of receiving his grace. The disciplines allow us to place ourselves before God so that he can transform us.

RICHARD FOSTER

Sola Gratia[11]

Before exploring the topic of spiritual disciplines, I'd like to take you on a little theological side trip. In writing a rule of life, or approaching any endeavor of the spiritual life, we want to emphasize the centrality of grace. Grace is an outpouring of God's loving-kindness that characterizes the grand story he's been writing since before time began. We see this grace from God's sweeping work of creation, to the extravagant gift of Christ's incarnation, death, and resurrection, culminating in the magnificent re-creation and renewal of all things in Christ's Second Coming. Creation, The Fall, incarnation, re-creation, and renewal. This greater story, or meta-narrative, speaks of a personal God who lives in community, a God who creates a people to live in community with him. When they rebel against him, God enters into history to rescue his people and restore relationship with them.

What grace! God's story is *our* story. In this story we find the answers to our deepest questions of meaning, purpose, and belonging. God's story is The Story in which all our stories belong. We find identity and purpose as God's living icons created for relationship with our Creator, imaging him in the world through expressions of his loving-kindness, justice, and peace. But tragically, all the way back to the first humans, we've rebelled against God, estranging ourselves from God, one another, and all of creation (Gen. 3; Rom. 3:23). In this story we find Christ—our very life. For God responded to our open rebellion with grace, not condemnation. His Son freely gave his life to reconcile God the Creator and his beloved children (2 Cor. 5:18–19).

Through faith in Christ we find life through a new relationship with the triune God. We enter into the eternal loving communion of Father, Son, and Holy Spirit (John 17). This new relationship profoundly transforms us. God makes us new—renewed, re-created in Christ and progressively restored to the original glory of Christ's likeness.[12] It's quite extraordinary, but over time God gradually remakes us in the likeness of Christ. We become more fully human, as God intends us to be.

The Transforming Power of Grace

This mystery, this new divine/human union is the source and strength, the vitality of the spiritual life. I can't emphasize enough that the Christian life is not about self-improvement, working our way toward holiness, but intimate relationship with God that radically transforms us. Too often we make the Christian life about doing, our own strivings, but the Christian journey unfolds in life-changing relationship with God. God as Trinity, or community of mutually self-giving persons—Father, Son, and Spirit, both models and shapes our life, a life lived within the community of believers. As we participate in an enduring personal relationship with the triune God, increasingly loving, trusting, and depending on him for the resources we need for life and godliness (2 Pet. 1:3–4), God transforms us. We experience a sanctifying work of his grace—growth in virtue and likeness to Christ by the power of his indwelling Spirit. In relationship with God, we truly thrive.

Through the grace or new life imparted to us in a sustained relationship with God, he gradually reshapes us from the inside out. We find grace present in the life of a Christ-follower in two ways, both as God's "favorable disposition toward undeserving sinners and a transforming power in the soul."[13] We first experience God's grace when we receive Christ by faith, as God "reorients" us toward him. At conversion we receive "God's gift of a redirected life in union with God's purpose for life."[14] Second, through this new relationship with God we receive ongoing grace—"the healing, revitalizing, and strengthening grace of God that is needed to sustain our souls."[15] God's gracious ongoing presence in us transforms and reshapes us in likeness to Christ. God continually imparts to us "habitual grace . . . a new principle of life transforming the soul."[16]

We refer to the process by which God progressively forms us in holiness and likeness to Christ as spiritual formation. As Augustine of Hippo, Martin Luther, and other great theologians of the Christian faith observe and the scriptures affirm, our hearts incline toward loving the wrong things (Isa. 53:6; Rom. 3:23). Before we receive new life in Christ, we're turned hopelessly inward, *homo incurvatus in se*—beings turned in on ourselves. Spiritual formation is the lifelong process in which God gradually transforms Christ-followers, reorienting our attentions and affections with his own.

As we follow Christ in an intentional and sustained way, opening ourselves to the movement of his Spirit in our life, we find ourselves growing in relationship with God and increasingly pursuing his purposes in the world. We experience holistic transformation, an inward heart change manifesting in the way we live our lives. We see such life change in a growing love for God and others—a dying to self and living for Christ. They'll know we are

Christians by our love (John 13:35), a self-sacrificial love concerned with the well-being and flourishing of others.

Following in the way of Christ involves a mysterious interplay of divine and human action. This dynamic of the Christian life can be characterized as divine initiative and human response. God initiates and we respond. But even in our response, God's grace is active, enabling us to participate and cooperate with his will. God actively works to form us in the image of Christ, and through the empowering of his indwelling Spirit we respond in obedience to his initiatives for change in our life. The Apostle Paul exhorts us to cooperate with the Spirit (Gal. 5:16, 25) rather than quench or hinder the Spirit (1 Thess. 5:19).

With the enablement of God's grace, we make every effort toward Christlikeness because God works in us toward that objective (Phil. 2:12–13). Our destiny as Christ's followers is to be formed in his image (Rom. 8:29). And in the fullness of God's story, he promises to complete this work in us (Phil. 1:6). Christ loves us and gave himself for us *so that we could be sanctified*—made holy, made like him. One glorious day, Christ will present to the Father his bride the church, holy and blameless before him (Eph. 5:25–27). No matter how broken we seem right now, one glorious day all who follow Christ will stand before God in this way.

Spiritual Disciplines as a Means of Grace

Out of desire to grow in holiness and likeness to Christ, we can follow Christ's own practices—spiritual disciplines such as silence and solitude, prayer, fasting, sacrifice, or scripture meditation. These practices give us opportunity to respond to Jesus' invitation to draw near to him and follow his way of life. For centuries the historic church has recognized spiritual disciplines as life-giving practices—means through which our Lord offers daily strength and sustenance for our souls.

Through spiritual disciplines we relate to God, who is both personal and intentional. These ancient practices provide a means of nurturing and attending to our relationship with God. "God has given us the disciplines of the spiritual life as a means of receiving his grace. The disciplines allow us to place ourselves before God so that he can transform us."[17]

Practicing spiritual disciplines with some consistency offers opportunity for us to grow in awareness of God's Spirit. In an increasingly complex and busy world, spiritual disciplines provide space for noticing God. "We attempt to focus more attention on God and less on other things that crowd into our hearts, minds, and lives by setting aside time and space just for God. The practices themselves have no particular power or goodness, but we hope that the Holy Spirit will use them to enable us to see God, culture, our families, and ourselves from God's perspective and help us be awake and attentive to God."[18] Spiritual disciplines can help us better attend and respond to God's active and abiding presence in our lives.

Richard Foster describes spiritual disciplines as the "path of disciplined grace" lying between two extremes. The path follows a long, narrow ridge which drops off precipitously on each side.

> Picture a long, narrow ridge with a sheer drop-off on either side. The chasm to the right is the way of moral bankruptcy through human strivings for righteousness. Historically this has been called the heresy of moralism. The chasm to the left is moral bankruptcy through the absence of human strivings. This has been called the heresy of antinomianism. On the ridge there is a path, the Disciplines of the spiritual life. This path leads to the inner transformation and healing for which we seek. . . . We must always remember that the path does not produce the change; it only places us where the change can occur.[19]

In regard to spiritual disciplines we can err in one of two ways. At one extreme, we can see such practices as a means of achieving our own righteousness—earning God's favor or approval through our own efforts or performance. This approach reveals a misunderstanding of our faith relationship with God. Moralism disregards the efficacy of Christ's sacrifice, the gift of God's grace which has already brought us into restored relationship with the Father. We don't need to strive through disciplines or other means to merit God's favor. Christ has reconciled us to God. Nothing can separate us from the love of God in Christ Jesus our Lord (Rom. 8:38–39).

At the same time, we err in the other extreme when we make no effort to follow the ways of our Lord. This contradicts Christ himself, "If anyone wishes to come after Me, he must deny himself, and take up his cross daily and follow Me" (Luke 9:23). Out of love, we make every effort to follow Christ and live in a way that pleases him. The Apostle Paul exhorts his young protégé Timothy to "Train yourself to be godly. For physical training is of some value, but godliness has value for all things, holding promise for both the present life and the life to come" (1 Tim. 4:7–8). As we've noted, effort holds a legitimate place in the Christian life, *but not earning*. As Dallas Willard aptly observes, "grace isn't opposed to effort, but earning."

Spiritual disciplines fall in one of two categories: practices of abstinence and practices of engagement. In practices of abstinence we abstain in some way from what we generally regard as legitimate desires. These disciplines include solitude, silence, fasting, or rest. We practice disciplines of abstinence to counteract sins of commission (doing what we should not do).[20] We periodically withdraw from a particular activity—fellowship, speaking, eating, or working—which may have gained too much importance in our lives.

Second, practices of engagement include disciplines we intentionally undertake as regular rhythms or habits. These include worship, scripture meditation, fixed-hour prayer, spiritual friendship, or giving. We practice disciplines of engagement to counteract sins of omission (not doing what we should do).[21] Out of our desire to draw near to Christ, to grow in virtue and likeness to him, we can follow the rhythms and practices of his life.

Spiritual Discipline 1
Scripture Meditation

But his delight is in the law of the LORD,
And in His law he meditates day and night.
He will be like a tree firmly planted by streams of water,
Which yields its fruit in its season
And its leaf does not wither;
And in whatever he does, he prospers.

PSALM 1:2–3

Let the word of Christ richly dwell within you.

COLOSSIANS 3:16

Come to the table and eat this book, for every word
in the book is intended to do something in us, give
health and wholeness, vitality and holiness to our soul
and body.

EUGENE PETERSON

The scriptures inform all aspects of monastic life. In addition to gathering eight times a day for corporate prayer, individual monks spend several hours each day in scripture meditation (*lectio divina* or divine reading). The Bible upholds the practice of meditating on God's word (or delighting in his law) as the way of flourishing and well-being.[22] For example, when Joshua assumes leadership from Moses, God instructs him to meditate on scripture. "This book of the law shall not depart from your mouth, but you shall meditate on it day and night, so that you may be careful to do according to all that is written in it; for then you will make your way prosperous, and then you will have success" (Josh. 1:8). Quite simply, meditating on God's Word brings life. We meditate on the scriptures to know God's ways and follow them.

What does it mean to meditate on the scriptures? Scripture meditation involves a "willingness to read slowly, hungrily, attentively, prayerfully, with the full expectation that there is a word in the text—an inspired word spoken by the eternal Word made flesh—that is to be believed, obeyed, hugged, devoured, as if all of one's life depended on it."[23] More than reading, we *feed* on God's word like an elaborate feast. We read slowly, hungrily, attentively, prayerfully, and expectantly—anticipating a personal encounter with the living God who inhabits his Word. With God's help, we fully embrace that received Word and wholeheartedly take it into our life.

First, we read slowly. For a period of time, we intentionally step out of our normal "hurry up" lives to linger, savor, and delight in God's personal Word to us. We resist the impulse to shift to something else in the middle of a page. We stay with it. We wait. We listen. This practice so sharply contrasts our 21st century life of fast food and instant downloads, that we may need to start with brief periods of daily meditation and work up to longer periods.

The great 19th century preacher Charles Haddon Spurgeon encourages us to regularly meditate on scripture or "muse on the things of God."

> We should be better Christians if we were more alone, waiting upon God, and gathering through meditation on his Word spiritual strength for labor in his service. We ought to muse upon the things of God, because we thus get the real nutriment out of them. Truth is something like the cluster of the vine: if we would have wine from it, we must bruise it; we must press and squeeze it many times. . . . So we must, by meditation, tread the clusters of truth, if we would get the wine of consolation therefrom.[24]

Meditating on scripture, "treading the clusters of truth," strengthens, nourishes, and enlightens our soul. "We must press and squeeze it many times," Spurgeon reminds us. Truly taking the word of God into our lives in such a way takes time—time to read, to listen, to pray, and to assimilate it into our daily thoughts and practices. The emphasis here is on slowing down long enough to hear God speak into our life through his Word.

Second, we read hungrily. In *Eat This Book*, Eugene Peterson defines scripture meditation as "dog-with-a-bone" reading.[25] The Hebrew word *hagah* is often translated as "meditate" (Ps. 1:2). But in Isaiah 31:4 *hagah* translates "growls" ("like a young lion growling over its prey").[26] *Hagah* is an onomatopoetic word, meaning "to meditate, moan, growl, utter, speak," and reflects the sighs and low moans made while one is pondering as the ancients practiced it.[27] "There is a certain kind of writing that invites this kind of reading," Peterson suggests, "soft purrs and low growls as we taste and savor, anticipate and take in the sweet and spicy, mouth-watering and soul-energizing morsel words—'O taste and see that the LORD is good!'" (Ps. 34:8).[28] As the personal, inspired, and living word of God to us, the scriptures are uniquely worthy of our slowing down to savor and enjoy.

Third, in scripture meditation we read attentively. We lay aside the distractions of everyday life and focus our attentions on God's Word to hear his voice. We don't multitask. We focus and attend to the scriptures. We ignore urges to email, text, call, or tweet. We become fully present to the God who is always fully present with us.

Fourth, we read prayerfully, asking God by his Spirit to direct and use the time we engage in his Word with heart, soul, and mind. We pray that he aligns our hearts with his. We pray that he brings about needed change in us as we encounter him in his Word.

Finally, we read expectantly, knowing that God indwells and moves through the scriptures in very personal and intimate ways. Mid-20th-century martyr Dietrich Bonhoeffer suggests, "In our meditation we ponder the chosen text on the strength of the promise that it has something utterly personal to say to us for this day and for our Christian life, that it is not only God's Word for the Church, but also God's Word for us individually."[29] With eager expectation and hope we approach the scriptures.

On the whole, scripture meditation allows for a very personal and life-giving encounter with the living God. In scripture meditation, we prayerfully (1) *observe* the passage (what does it say?), (2) *interpret* the passage (what does it mean?) and (3) *apply* the truth of what we encounter (how can I live this truth?). We might ask ourselves, what do I learn about God in this text? What do I learn about myself? How can I respond to this Word?

We meditate on scripture for transformation. We read God's Word to encounter the Author and become more like him. "We are reading to be changed, to be transformed, to be recreated, to be reshaped ever more fully into the image of the Word incarnate, Jesus Christ our Lord, sent by the Father to redeem and recreate."[30] We read to become who God intends us to be in Christ.

Practicing Scripture Meditation: More than a method, we can think of scripture meditation in terms of *dwelling*. The Apostle Paul exhorts us to let the word of Christ "richly dwell" within us (Col. 3:16). Our words and deeds flow from those places where our minds consistently dwell, from what we tend to meditate on and think about. So before practicing the discipline of scripture meditation this week, take time for self-examination. Prayerfully examine what you tend to "feed" on. Are there particular media—music, television shows, or websites that you regularly consume? Where does your mind tend to dwell and what tends to dwell in you? What are you inclined to think about or talk about?

Second, choose several verses or a short passage on which to meditate this week. Some view the practice of *lectio divina* as a four-step process—not in a linear sense, but more like a dance—the steps overlapping and overflowing into one another. We can loosely outline the four steps as:

1. Reading the passage slowly, listening for a particular word or phrase that stands out to you.

2. Reflecting on the passage, particularly the word or phrase that seems directed at you (like Peterson's dog gnawing on a bone).

3. Responding with prayer to the passage.

4. Resting in the presence of God with his Word.

Be prepared to share your experience with your Thrive Group.

Notes

1. Benedict of Nursia, *The Rule of Saint Benedict*, Vintage Spiritual Classics (New York: Vintage Books, 1998), 12. In the remainder of this book, *The Rule of St. Benedict* will be referred to as *RB*.

2. Terrence Kardong, "Work Is Prayer: Not!" *Assumption Abbey Newsletter*, October 1995; available from http://www.osb.org/gen/topics/work/kard1.html.

3. Terrence Kardong, "Work Is Prayer: Not!" *Assumption Abbey Newsletter*, October 1995; available from http://www.osb.org/gen/topics/work/kard1.html.

4. For this introduction to culture, I've drawn from my friend Dr. Barry Jones' lectures in, "Spiritual Formation in Contemporary Culture" at Dallas Theological Seminary, 2012.

5. Philip Kenneson, *Life on the Vine* (Downers Grove: IVP, 1999), 26-27.

6. Ibid, 29.

7. Ibid.

8. Ibid.

9. Thomas Moore, Preface, *The Rule of St. Benedict*, Vintage Spiritual Classics (Collegeville, MN: Vintage Books, 1998), xvi-xvii.

10. The question format is adapted from the Spiritual Formation curriculum at Dallas Theological Seminary of which I was a contributor.

11. The Latin, *sola gratia*, means grace alone and is associated with Protestant Reformers like Martin Luther, who emphasized that the whole of the spiritual life is empowered and enabled by God's grace.

12. "Therefore if anyone is in Christ, he is a new creature; the old things passed away; behold, new things have come (2 Cor. 5:17)." Jesus forgives our sins and invites us into a new relationship with him by faith, a relationship through which God progressively restores Christ's image and likeness in us. God loves the people he created. He gave his Son so that "whoever believes in him should not perish, but have eternal life (John 3:16)." In this book those who believe in Christ and follow him as Lord and Savior are referred to as Christ-followers.

13. Simon Chan, *Spiritual Theology*, (Downers Grove: InterVarsity Press, 1999), 89.

14. Robert Webber, *The Divine Embrace*, (Grand Rapids: Baker, 2006), 16.

15. James C. Wilhoit, *Spiritual Formation as if the Church Mattered*, (Grand Rapids: Baker, 2006), 57.

16. Chan, 89.

17. Richard Foster, *Celebration of Discipline* (New York: HarperCollins, 1998), 7.

18. Jeannette Bakke, *Holy Invitations* (Grand Rapids, MI: Baker Books, 2000), 231.

19. Foster, 8.

20. Dallas Willard, *The Spirit of the Disciplines* (New York: HarperCollins, 1988), 159.

21. Ibid.

22. For example, see Psalms 1:1-3; 48:9; 77:12; 119:15, 27, 48, 95 and 148.

23. Christopher Hall, "Reading Christ in the Heart," in *Life in the Spirit*, ed. J. Greenman and G. Kalantzis (Downers Grove: InterVarsity, 2007), 144.

24. Charles H. Spurgeon, *Morning and Evening: Daily Readings,* Christian Classics Ethereal Library; available from http://www.ccel.org/ccel/spurgeon/morneve.d1012am.html.

25. Eugene Peterson, *Eat This Book* (Grand Rapids: Eerdmans, 2006), 4.

26. Ibid., 2.

27. W. E. Vine, Merrill Unger and William White, *Vine's Complete Expository Dictionary of Old and New Testament Words* (Nashville: Thomas Nelson, 1985) 150.

28. Peterson, 2.

29. Dietrich Bonhoeffer, *Life Together* (USA: Harper and Row, 1954), 82.

30. Hall, 144.

CHAPTER 2

Fidelity to Christ

Let us hold fast to the confession of our hope without wavering, for he who has promised is faithful.

HEBREWS 10:23

Let them prefer nothing whatever to Christ, and may he bring us all together to everlasting life.

BENEDICT OF NURSIA

We find an overarching theme in the *Rule of St. Benedict* in the old-fashioned word fidelity. Benedict's life and writings evidence a sincere desire to live a devout and holy life, a life in imitation of Christ's faithfulness. Upon entrance into the monastic community, new members vow fidelity, stability, and obedience (*RB* 58). First, they pledge fidelity, or "faithfulness to a person, cause, or belief, demonstrated by continuing loyalty and support."[1] In the case of the Benedictine monks, they promise faithfulness to Christ, to the monastic way of life, and to helping one another live holy and virtuous lives. The second vow of stability sets the Benedictines apart, and is likely why these monastic communities endure when others do not. With the vow of stability, initiates pledge faithfulness to a particular monastic community for life. Over a lifetime, this demand for stability requires additional virtues such as humility, patience, and longsuffering. Finally, they pledge obedience to God, the scriptures, their communal rule, the abbot and others in authority, and one another.

We find these themes of faithfulness and devotion to Christ in earlier monastic rules such as that of the great theologian Augustine of Hippo (354–430), the founder of monasticism in northern Africa. In 397 AD Augustine wrote a brief rule, the *Praeceptum,* for a small community he oversaw in the city of Hippo. Dubbed a kind of "urban monasticism,"[2] Augustine's rule is characterized by love, communal living, shared property, mutual accountability, discipline, and moderation. The community emphasized concern for the common good above one's own. Augustine's rule greatly influenced Benedict, who picks up on many of these themes. For Augustine, their purpose for living in community was mutual devotion to God. "In the first place—and this is the very reason for your being gathered together as one—you should live in the house in unity of spirit and you should have one soul and one heart centered on God" (*Pr* 1.2).[3]

Love for Christ inspires such fidelity. Our growing love for Christ compels us to live for him. Benedict reminds us that, for those who choose to live in the monastic way, the motivation is simply love. God's love prompts our love (1 John 4:19). God's faithfulness prompts our faithfulness. "It is love that impels them to pursue everlasting life; therefore, they are eager to take the narrow road of which the Lord says: Narrow is the road that leads to life. They no longer live by their own judgment, giving in to their whims and appetites; rather they walk according to another's decisions and directions, choosing to live in monasteries and to have an abbot over them" (*RB* 5). Because of their love and gratitude for Christ, they choose the narrow road—the way of discipline, obedience, and self-giving. "The road that leads to life."

Fidelity in the Scriptures

We don't need to look far for examples of fidelity in the scriptures—Noah, Abraham, Sarah, Moses, Joshua, Rahab, and David to name a few (see Heb. 11). Abraham, the great patriarch of Israel, exhibits great faithfulness, obeying God's call to leave his home and follow him (Gen. 12:1–3). Remarkably, Abraham responds to God's invitation, "not knowing where he was going" (Heb. 11:8).

God establishes a covenant agreement with Abraham, promising to bless him and make him a great nation. Eventually, God promises to establish this covenant through Abraham's long-awaited son Isaac. But in what must have been a deeply troubling time for Abraham, God directs him to sacrifice his son. With characteristic faith Abraham sets out early in the morning for Mount Moriah, the place of sacrifice. As they walk, Abraham assures his son, "God will provide for Himself the burnt offering" (Gen. 22:8). And indeed God proves faithful, providing the sacrifice he requires and sparing Isaac. Here we find a timeless truth. God provides what he requires of us. Abraham's sense of this truth undergirds his faith.

Through one man's faith, blessings abound to many. God explains to Abraham, "in your seed all the nations of the earth shall be blessed, *because you have obeyed My voice*" (Gen. 22:18, emphasis added). Jesus the Savior, the hope of the world, is the promised seed descended of Abraham through his son Isaac. God's gracious act of provision on Mount Moriah foreshadows the most extravagant grace in all of history. Several thousands of years later, God provides the sacrifice he requires for our forgiveness. In sacrificing his only Son, God provides the needed sacrifice for the sins of the whole world. A remarkable gift reconciling God and mankind.

Fidelity Today

As Christ-followers today we depend on the empowerment of God's Spirit to walk faithfully in the large and small. Around the world we find extraordinary examples of fidelity. In 2014, in the Islamic country of Sudan, a judge sentenced a 26-year-old pregnant woman named Meriam Ibrahim to 100 lashes and execution by hanging for apostasy (abandoning Islam). The judge found Meriam guilty of adultery because she was married to a Christian with whom she shared one child and was pregnant with another.

Even in light of this devastating sentence, Meriam refused to renounce her Christian beliefs. Upon reflection, one Anglican bishop observed, Meriam "is navigating according to biblical fidelity, and one can also well imagine, according to the demonstrated faithfulness that Jesus Christ has manifest in her life. He must be real and 'tried and true' in her life for her to be committed to Him even to the point of death."[4] As our relationship with Jesus deepens, becoming "real and tried and true," he may call us to increasing levels of faithfulness. We can draw strength from the unparalleled fidelity of our Lord and the example of the faithful followers who've gone before us.

Fidelity in a Culture Inclined toward Infidelity

In some segments of the predominant culture, the virtue of fidelity seems scarce, almost old-fashioned. Overall, we seem to find ourselves in a culture characterized by diminishing loyalties. Our fidelity falters under practices like "no-fault divorce," where neither party need provide a rationale for ending a marriage relationship. The percentage of married couples in our culture is declining. In 2010 married couples represented 48 percent of the households in the United States as compared to 78 percent in 1950.[5]

Our consumerist culture adds fuel to the fire. With an eye toward increasing market shares, advertisers encourage us to be "deeply committed to being uncommitted."[6] Through a daily barrage of ever-changing web ads customized to our likes and preferences (and often mined from our personal e-mails and online practices), advertisers promote dissatisfaction with the old and desire for the new. About the time we learn our way around the newest personal tech device, a newer release makes ours obsolete. As the pace of change accelerates, we can feel trapped in a perpetual game of "catch-up."

In fact, author Philip Kenneson observes that contemporary advertising practices "cultivate within us a paradoxical 'loyalty' to the transitory and fleeting."[7] In contrast to monastic virtues such as fidelity or stability, contemporary culture seems to uphold "virtues" of mobility and disposability, a surface or cursory kind of commitment. A "what's in it for me" kind of commitment. For Christ-followers the concern becomes the broader relational implications of such tendencies. Kenneson suggests that "A disposable culture might dispose us to avoid making commitments in the first place."[8] As a Thrive Group, this week we'll want to consider how cultural inclinations toward unfaithfulness might influence our own ability to maintain faithfulness, whether to the Lord or other people.

As Christ-followers striving for fidelity in a culture seemingly inclined to infidelity, we would do well to clarify our own values and loyalties. How would we describe what we personally value or find important? Where do our loyalties lie? And how do our personal values relate to either our cultural context or our identity as Christ's followers? As we've said, in some respects our prevailing culture may promote a different set of values, loyalties, and priorities than those upheld in the scriptures.

Often our individual values or guiding principles arise from our personal stories or life experiences so I encourage you to reflect a little on the origins of your deeply held values or convictions. Spend some time in prayer considering what's important to you and why that might be. How might your values relate to your life experiences, or the story God is writing in your life? For example, a young man deeply influenced by a youth pastor or coach may have a passion for investing in the lives of youth or college students. Or, a woman who experienced her parent's struggle with addiction may find herself passionately advocating for children or spouses of alcoholics. On the other hand, a woman who participated in vibrant Christian community as a child may carry a high value for authentic, loving relationships into whichever context she finds herself.

As we've said, each of us already lives in a particular way. Writing a rule of life offers a means of being more intentional about living in a way that reflects our beliefs, values, and priorities as followers of Christ. For example, in the pages of her personal journals, Susanna Wesley, devout mother of John and Charles Wesley, thoughtfully examines the pattern of her daily life. She vows "Never to spend more time in any matter of mere recreation in one day than I spend in private religious duties."[9] This week as you examine your own way of life, you'll want to carefully consider how well the pattern of your daily life reflects your personal beliefs and values.

A More Life-Giving Way

In the last chapter you identified several personally significant scriptures which might form a foundation or vision for your rule or way of life. This week you'll want to identify five or six core values or deeply held beliefs that drive you. What might be the origins of your convictions or guiding principles? In what ways could your daily life better reflect what's important to you? Finally, in keeping with our chapter theme, you'll want to consider in what ways God might be personally inviting you to fidelity in Christ.

Questions for Reflection and Discussion

1. **Reflect on the Word**

   Identify a person in scripture that demonstrates fidelity toward God. In what ways do they exhibit faithfulness?

   ....

   ....

   ....

2. **Reflect on our world**

   Does the predominant culture in which you live value or promote fidelity or loyalty? If so, to what or to whom are you encouraged to show faithfulness? In what ways does your culture discourage the virtue of fidelity?

   ....

   ....

   ....

What values are dominant in your culture? In what ways do these values align with or work against biblical values such as fidelity to Christ?

....

....

....

3. **Reflect on your spiritual journey**

Looking back at your own spiritual journey, in whom have you seen fidelity to Christ modeled? In what ways was it modeled? How did it impact you?

....

....

....

4. **Reflect on your rule of life**

List five or six of your core values or deeply held convictions or beliefs. How might they relate to your personal story or experiences?

....

....

....

How might your daily life more truly reflect these values?

....

....

....

5. **This week, complete Spiritual Discipline 2: Silence and Solitude.**

Spiritual Discipline 2
Silence and Solitude

When I am still, compulsion (the busyness that Hilary of Tours called "a blasphemous anxiety to do God's work for Him") gives way to compunction (being pricked or punctured). That is, God can break through the many layers with which I protect myself, so that I can hear His word and be poised to listen.

LEIGHTON FORD

In his earthly ministry, we find our Lord practicing silence and solitude with some regularity. In the intensity of ministry, Jesus often withdraws to a lonely place to pray (Luke 5:16–17). With many needs pressing upon him, Jesus sees the need to retreat in solitude to pray and commune with his Father. What are these disciplines about? Why did Christ make this a priority?

The practices of solitude and silence involve periodically withdrawing from others to be with God in silence and quietness of soul. In solitude and silence God invites us to lay down our busyness, our compulsions, our own ways of trying to "make life work." In solitude and silence God invites us to be still, to cease our striving, and rest in who he is (Ps. 46:10).

Solitude and silence are often practiced together. But these disciplines emphasize inner disposition more than place or people. "Solitude is more a state of mind and heart than it is a place. . . . Crowds, or the lack of them, have little to do with this inward attentiveness. It is quite possible to be a desert hermit and never experience solitude."[10]

We can practice solitude either alone or with others, for it involves cultivating inner stillness or "deep inner silence." Allowing ourselves to reach this place of quiet provides opportunity to listen and receive, to discern the "gentle blowing" of the Spirit of God in our life (1 Kings 19:9–13). Allowing ourselves to settle into such stillness equips us both for solitude and the company of others. We become more keenly aware of God's presence and voice.

> If we possess inward solitude we do not fear being alone, for we know that we are not alone. Neither do we fear being with others, for they do not control us. In the midst of noise and confusion we are settled into a deep inner silence. Whether alone or among people, we always carry with us a portable sanctuary of the heart.[11]

The disciplines of solitude and silence offer great benefit. Nonetheless, many of us struggle to find inner stillness. Especially in today's world, numerous things vie for our attention. It may take time to disentangle or disengage ourselves. Centuries ago, Basil of Caesarea (329–379) confides his own struggles to his friend Gregory of Nazianzus.

> What I do myself, day and night, in this remote spot, I am ashamed to write. I have abandoned my life in town, as one sure to lead to countless ills, but I have not been able to get quiet of myself. . . . I carry my own troubles with me. . . . So, in the end, I have not got much good out of my solitude. What I ought to have done, what would have enabled me to keep close to the footprints of Him who has led the way to salvation . . . is this. We must strive after a quiet mind.[12]

Even in the remoteness of Basil's location, he brings his troubles with him, finding himself "distracted by a thousand worldly cares."[13] As for many of us, although solitude removes some distractions, Basil struggles with the greatest of them, "getting quiet of himself." He discovers that to encounter God in a meaningful way, we must "strive after a quiet mind."

Thomas à Kempis belonged to an Augustinian monastic community near Zwolle, Germany. In 1413 he wrote a guide to cultivating the spiritual life that has become a devotional classic. In *The Imitation of Christ*, he notes that in silence and solitude we often discover what we miss in the company of others. "Within your cell you will discover what you will only too often lose abroad. . . . In silence and quietness the devout soul makes progress and learns the hidden mysteries of the Scriptures. . . . For the further she withdraws from the tumult of the world, the nearer she draws to her Maker."[14] In imitation of our Lord, God invites us to regularly "withdraw from the tumult of the world" and draw near to him.

God communicates in countless ways. Our role is to cultivate better awareness. Regularly practicing this listening posture of silence and solitude can help us better attend to God's loving presence in our life. We practice silence and solitude, quietness and stillness before God, to listen to him. We practice these disciplines to cultivate a deeper awareness of the many ways in which God continually speaks into our lives.

Quite simply, we practice these disciplines for the sake of our soul. We enter into silence to listen to Christ's voice, find refreshment in his presence and receive life. We bring this renewed life back into the rest of our day, into our work and recreation and relationships. Christ invites the weary and over-burdened to find rest in relationship with him (Matt. 11:28). The demands of 21st century life can deplete and exhaust us. Regularly following our Lord in rhythms of silence and solitude offers needed renewal and restoration.

A final and rarely sought purpose of solitude and silence is struggle. Sometimes the process of *disengaging* from other aspects of life proves tremendously difficult. But an additional reason for these disciplines is to examine our heart, to discover those places where we're pursuing things of our own making rather than God's. And as we see the reality of our soul condition, we bring it before God and allow his grace and mercy to wash over us. We rest in the presence of who God is, of what he has already done to forgive and reconcile us to him, and of what he is presently doing to make us into a people that reflect Christ's image to the world.

> In solitude I get rid of my scaffolding: no friends to talk with, no telephone calls to make, no meetings to attend, no music to entertain, no books to distract, just me—naked, vulnerable, weak, sinful, deprived, broken—nothing. . . . The task is to persevere in my solitude, to stay in my cell until all my seductive visitors get tired of pounding on my door and leave me alone. . . . The struggle is real because the danger is real. It is the danger of living the whole of our life as one long defense against the reality of our condition."[15]

As painful as it can be to see "the reality of our condition," it's vital to the health of our soul. In our willingness to see, we take the first step toward change. Though daunting, solitude helps us discern the condition of our soul—the needs, longings, or inclinations that we've stuffed beneath the surface. We ask for help where we feel depleted. We confess where we fall short. In our time of need we bring these things before God and receive his abundant mercy, grace, and healing.

We all live full lives and may not be able to get away for extended silence or retreat. Richard Foster encourages us to take advantage of the "little solitudes" in our day. "These tiny snatches of time are often lost to us. What a pity! They can and should be redeemed. They are times for inner quiet, for reorienting our lives like a compass needle. They are little moments that help us to be genuinely present where we are."[16] Foster urges us to take advantage of daily little opportunities to reorient our hearts toward a loving God and live fully in the moment.

Practicing silence and solitude: This week, block out some extended time to practice silence and solitude (at least one hour, more if you are familiar with this practice). Schedule some time to ride a bike trail or walk along a lake, to visit an art museum, a retreat center or your own backyard—somewhere that refreshes your soul and allows you the time and space to be quiet and alone with God. Feel free to journal any thoughts, prayers, or feelings that surface. Be prepared to share your experience with your Thrive Group. What was it like for you to be quiet and still before God? What struggles did you experience? What insights did you gain?

Notes:

1. Fidelity, *Oxford Dictionaries*, Oxford University Press; available at http://oxforddictionaries.com/us/definition/american_english/fidelity?q=fidelity.

2. Gerald Bonner, *Saint Augustine: The Monastic Rules*, The Augustine Series, Vol. IV (Hyde Park, N.Y.: New City Press, 2004), 12.

3. Ibid., 110. Please note: in the remainder of this book the *Praeceptum* will be referred to as *Pr.*

4. Excerpted from the email newsletter *GlobalView*, distributed May 2014 by Bishop Bill Atwood of the International Diocese of the ACNA (Anglican Church in North America).

5. http://www.nytimes.com/2011/05/26/us/26marry.html?_r=0

6. Kenneson, 185.

7. Ibid.

8. Ibid., 187.

9. Charles Bullock, *Our Own Fireside* (London: James Nisbitt and Co., 1871) 235.

10. Foster, *Celebration*, 96-97.

11. Ibid.

12. Basil of Caesarea, *Letter 2 to Gregory of Nazianzus*, The St. Pachomius Orthodox Library, Sept-Oct 1995; available at http://www.voskrese.info/spl/basil2.html#2.

13. Ibid.

14. Thomas à Kempis, *The Imitation of Christ*, Trans. by Leo Sherley-Price (London: Penguin Books, 1952). In the remainder of this curriculum, *The Imitation of Christ* will be referred to as *IC*.

15. Henri Nouwen, *The Way of the Heart* (New York: HarperCollins, 1991), 27-28.

16. Foster, *Celebration,* 106.

CHAPTER 3

Attending to Our Relationship with Christ

> Earth's crammed with heaven, and every common
> bush afire with God; but only he who sees takes off his
> shoes—the rest sit round it and pluck blackberries.
>
> ELIZABETH BARRETT BROWNING

> But he who enters by the door is the shepherd of the
> sheep...The sheep hear his voice, and he calls his own
> sheep by name and leads them out. When he has
> brought out all his own, he goes before them, and the
> sheep follow him, for they know his voice.
>
> JOHN 10:2–4

Our relationship with the Good Shepherd is at the heart of our walk of faith. Like sheep listening for their shepherd's voice, Christ invites us to listen closely, to pay attention to the ways he's present and working in our daily lives. Christ leads the way and Christ enables us to follow. Another emphasis found in monastic rules is listening—cultivating close attention to God's abiding presence in our lives. Step by step. Day by day.

This doesn't come easily. But monastic life is crafted with intentionality. The Benedictines follow a certain order, rhythm, and way of life designed to support their common desire to follow Christ. A devout and loving community provides the context. "The workshop where we are

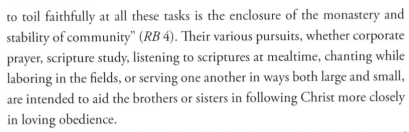

to toil faithfully at all these tasks is the enclosure of the monastery and stability of community" (*RB* 4). Their various pursuits, whether corporate prayer, scripture study, listening to scriptures at mealtime, chanting while laboring in the fields, or serving one another in ways both large and small, are intended to aid the brothers or sisters in following Christ more closely in loving obedience.

From the opening lines of his rule, Benedict emphasizes this theme of listening. "Listen carefully, my son, to the master's instructions and attend to them with the ear of your heart. This is advice from a father who loves you; welcome it, and faithfully put it into practice" (*RB* Prologue). Benedict urges his followers to listen well, "with the ear of your heart," and receive his advice. He advises us to abandon the self-will and trust in God for the grace we need to follow him.

"What, dear brothers," Benedict asks, "is more delightful than this voice of the Lord calling to us" (*RB* Prologue)? Like the sheep in John 10, in faith we follow Christ because we know his voice. We know his nature and character. We know the delight of following him. He calls us by name and leads us out. He goes before us and we follow. We listen to him and do as he does. In Benedict's words we find a picture of the intimate and enduring relationship of Psalm 23. When we walk daily with Christ, we exclaim with the psalmist, "surely goodness and mercy shall follow me all the days of my life" (Ps. 23:6). In trust we lean on Christ—daily listening and depending on him to lead, feed, restore, sustain, and care for us every step of the way.

Throughout his earthly life, Jesus consistently lives this example of close communion with God the Father. In fact, Jesus chooses to live in a relationship of humble dependence on the Father. In this self-limiting relationship, Jesus the Son can do nothing of himself (John 5:19). The Son does as the Father does. Jesus came not to do his own will, but the will of the one who sent him (John 6:38). Jesus models submission to the Father's will in his earnest prayer at the Garden of Gethsemane just before his arrest and crucifixion. "Father, if You are willing, remove this cup from me; yet not my will, but yours be done" (Luke 22:41).

Jesus characterizes his relationship with the Father as abiding—I in him and he in me. "Do you not believe that I am in the Father, and the Father is in me? The words that I say to you I do not speak on my own initiative, but the Father abiding in me does his works" (John 14:10). Here Jesus offers a model to follow in our relationship with him—moment by moment dependence. We can cultivate this habit of dependence, of close attention, as a daily discipline. Like a compass needle continually reorienting northward, we turn to Jesus again and again. How is God at work in my life and how can I follow?

Jesus offers the metaphor of a grapevine to explain to his disciples what it means to abide in him. "I am the vine, you are the branches; he who abides in Me and I in him, he bears much fruit, for apart from me you can do nothing" (John 15:5). To abide in Christ means to depend on him like branches depend on the grapevine for sustenance and life. Like the relationship of Father and Son, apart from Christ we cannot bear fruit that glorifies God (John 15:8). If we rely on Christ in this way, we bear the fruit of his Spirit—love, joy, peace, patience, kindness, goodness, faithfulness, gentleness, and self-control (Gal. 5:22–23).

The Greek word for 'abide' (*meno*) refers to "an inward, enduring personal communion."[1] Life for a follower of Jesus means staying as close to him as possible. Through relationship with him, Jesus gives us the resources we need for life and godliness (2 Pet. 1:2–3). As Jesus models in relationship with the Father, apart from an intimate relationship with him we'll never flourish. Apart from an intimate relationship with Jesus we'll never become who God truly intends for us to be. Again we see the vitality, the life-giving quality of relationship with God. We live the abundant life, we thrive "by nourishing ourselves constantly on his personal presence."[2]

Learning to Pay Attention

Our attentiveness to God fosters and deepens our relationship with him. God invites us to seek his presence always (Ps. 105:4). We must listen well and learn to pay attention to his presence and the leading of his Spirit in our lives. In Exodus 3:1–6 we find an example of Moses' attentiveness to God.

> Now Moses was pasturing the flock of Jethro his father-in-law, the priest of Midian; and he led the flock to the west side of the wilderness and came to Horeb, the mountain of God. The angel of the Lord appeared to him in a blazing fire from the midst of a bush; and he looked, and behold, the bush was burning with fire, yet the bush was not consumed. So Moses said, "I must turn aside now and see this marvelous sight, why the bush is not burned up." When the Lord saw that he turned aside to look, God called to him from the midst of the bush and said, "Moses, Moses!" And he said, "Here I am." Then He said, "Do not come near here; remove your sandals from your feet, for the place on which you are standing is holy ground." He said also, "I am the God of your father, the God of Abraham, the God of Isaac, and the God of Jacob."

Having fled Egypt, at this point Moses has lingered forty years in the Sinai wilderness. But one day, while tending Jethro's flocks he notices something unusual. *When God sees that Moses turns aside to look*, he calls to Moses (Ex 3:4). This encounter with God becomes a holy and pivotal moment in the life of Moses and all of Israel. What would have happened if Moses had not turned aside to look? What opportunities for the Lord's guidance and direction do we miss because of distraction or self-focus? Remarkably, over time Moses' relationship with God develops and deepens to the point where God speaks to Moses "face to face, just as a man speaks to his friend" (Ex. 33:11).

How did Moses get to a place of such intimacy with God? How can we get there? For starters, we need to slow down enough to pay attention to what God is doing in our lives. We need to set aside distractions, even good things, which get in the way of our following closely after him. Are there some good, even legitimate aspects of your life that Christ invites you to set aside for a while? Francois Fenelon, 17th century mystic, reminds us that, "Christ, the eternal Word, who must be communicated to the soul to give it new life, requires the most intense attention to his voice. . . . We must forget ourselves, and all self-interest, and listen and be attentive to God."[3] This ancient sage reminds us that to follow Christ closely, we must practice the ancient discipline of "self-forgetfulness" and listen. As we sincerely desire to attend more closely to God's voice, we can look to the Spirit of God to foster that awareness. And as we grow in Christ, he invites us not only to a deeper awareness of him, but also to deeper self-awareness. The two "knowings" are intertwined.

How Is It with Your Soul?

The Methodist movement began in the 18th century when John and Charles Wesley founded the Holy Club at Oxford. This group of friends met weekly to support each other in living a devout and holy life. They received the label of "methodist" because they emphasized method and rule in their preaching. Those who responded to their preaching were organized into "societies." Societies were divided into smaller classes which served as discipleship, accountability, or support groups. Each group meeting began with the question, "How is it with your soul?"

Before we explore the question of how it is with your soul, we must first ask, what is the soul? Without getting too in-depth here, we can think of the soul as an immaterial part of our being, that aspect of one's person that interrelates the components of a human person—mind, body, emotions, and spirit (or will).[4] Since the soul is integrative in nature, we sometimes refer to the whole human person as a soul. The writers of scripture often use the term soul in this broader sense (e.g., in the Psalms). Sometimes, we see the terms soul and spirit used interchangeably in the scriptures (Luke 1:46–47), but though closely related, some distinction can be made (Heb. 4:12). God designed us for relationship with him, and as integrated beings we respond to him holistically (with our mind, body, emotions, and spirit), but especially from the innermost place of our soul or spirit. For our purposes here, when we ask how it is with your soul, we are simply asking you to respond from a place of spiritual depth, thoughtfully, and truthfully.

So, how is it? How is it with your soul today? We observe a range of experiences of the soul in the raw honesty of the psalmists' cries before God. In the Psalms we find that our soul can delight (Ps. 94:19) or rejoice (Ps. 35:9). On the other hand, our soul can experience dismay (Ps. 6:3), grief (Ps. 31:9), or despair (Ps. 42). Our soul thirsts for God like a deer pants for water (Ps. 63) and our thirsty soul finds satisfaction in God (Ps. 107:9). In God the soul finds rest (Ps. 23:3), sustenance (Ps. 54:4), and healing from sin (Ps. 41:4). In the presence of God, David likens his soul to a weaned child resting against his mother, composed and quieted (Ps. 131:2).

As you reflect on the state of your soul, what do you notice? Perhaps you find yourself distracted, weary, or anxious. Jesus invites us to come to him and find rest for your soul (Matt. 11:29). Or perhaps you sense a need for simplicity or quiet or the companionship of a spiritual friend. As we discern the condition of our soul, we bring ourselves before God with the same authenticity and trust as the psalmists. The Lord our Shepherd knows well the inner workings of our soul. And the Lord our Shepherd restores our depleted soul. The ancient prayer of *examen*, discussed in Spiritual Discipline 3, offers a daily means of attending both to God's presence and to the condition of our soul.

Helping Others Pay Attention

As members of his church, God invites us to help each other pay attention, to prayerfully attend to the ongoing movement of his Spirit. Our delight as Christ-followers is in turning our attention to the ways in which God is *already at work* in the hearts and lives of his people. Eugene Peterson wisely suggests that our task is "not to get God to do something I think needs to be done, but to become aware of what God is doing so that I can respond to it and participate and take delight in it."[5] We find joy in discerning what

God is about, responding and participating in the work of God's grace in and around us.

When thinking about others, Peterson suggests we ask: "How can I be with them in such a way that they can become what God is making them?"[6] We can accompany others in noticing and responding to God's active grace in their lives. Eli fulfills this role in the boy Samuel's life (1 Sam. 3:1–10). In those days a word from the Lord was rare. One day the Lord calls Samuel three times, yet Samuel doesn't understand God's call. The elder Eli discerns that the Lord is calling and instructs Samuel accordingly. "'Go lie down, and it shall be if He calls you, that you shall say, 'Speak, Lord, for Your servant is listening'" (1 Sam. 3:9). The Lord calls Samuel again and this time Samuel responds. As we cultivate greater attentiveness in the body of Christ, we can support one another in discerning God's presence and movement.

Listen and Obey

In monastic life, listening ties closely to obedience. Benedictine monks seek to obey the scriptures, the precepts of their communal rule, the abbot, and others in authority. "A man submits to his superior in all obedience for the love of God, imitating the Lord, of whom the Apostle says: He became obedient even to death" (*RB* 7). They practice the discipline of obedience daily, not only out of love for Christ, but *as a way of training in obedience.* Additionally, Benedict exhorts the brothers or sisters to mutual obedience or submission. "Obedience is a blessing to be shown to all, not only to the abbot but also to one another as brothers, since we know that it is by this way of obedience that we go to God" (*RB* 71).

The Latin word for obedience, *oboedire,* means to hear or listen towards. Benedictine monks practice obedience as a way of cultivating attentiveness to God. "The practice of obedience is a means by which the monk cultivates an openness and responsiveness to a voice that is not his own, and in so doing grows a heart attuned to the voice of God."[7]

Obedience rests on the conviction of God's abiding presence with us. Obedience comes from an alertness or attentiveness to God's voice at all times, in all things. Obedience comes from an openness to God's voice, however he might speak to us. "Obedience for Benedict is the practice of leaning in with the ear of one's heart to listen for what God may be saying. . . . It is the practice of openly receiving and responding to another's perspective, counsel, or request with the understanding that God is present there."[8] Obedience manifests as we constantly listen for his voice with humble responsiveness. As we form the habit of listening and obeying others, we're more inclined to listen and obey God.

Paying Attention in a Culture Inclined to Inattention

A recent study conducted by the U.S. Center for Disease Control and Prevention indicates that a rising percentage of American children are diagnosed with Attention Deficit Hyperactivity Disorder (ADHD). ADHD is characterized by difficulty in sustaining attention, impulsivity, and hyperactivity.[9] Adults too frequently joke about our "ADD-ness." It seems that the ability to pay attention in a sustained way is becoming a lost art. We've grown accustomed to the constant interruption of cell phone calls, texts, tweets, and e-mails, whether checking out at the grocery store or driving a remote mountain pass. When asked to practice sustained silence or solitude, we struggle.

Are certain cultural practices exacerbating our ability to pay attention? Shane Hipps, in *Flickering Pixels: How Technology Shapes Your Faith*, seems to suggest just that. He observes the profoundly formative influence of the *media* through which we communicate, citing Marshall McLuhan's infamous notion that "the medium is the message."[10] In other words, the means by which we transmit a message or particular content bears enormous influence, more than the message itself. The predominant medium of television, for example, actually "*repatterns neural pathways in the brain*" (emphasis added).[11] These new neural pathways are "simply opposed to the pathways required for reading, writing, and sustained concentration."[12] Hipps likens the televised image to "brain candy" requiring no mental engagement or capacity. In contrast, the practice of reading offers "brain protein," demanding "concentration and sustained neural energy."[13] It is unclear what is causing the increased diagnosis of ADD and ADHD in America, but as we consider which daily practices to include in our rule of life, we would do well to reflect on how common, seemingly benign, cultural practices might add to our inattentiveness.

A More Life-Giving Way

This week you'll want to evaluate two aspects of attentiveness in your spiritual life—your ability to notice God's presence and your ability to notice what's going on with your own soul. In other words, we'll take time this week to discern both our depth of awareness of God's presence in our lives and our depth of self-awareness. Again I want to offer a word of encouragement. These disciplines of awareness do not come instantly. I encourage you to prayerfully begin where you are, to begin to notice God's presence in your days and begin to notice the ways in which you're responding to life in his presence. As always, God will supply what he asks of us. God will lead you in your journey toward greater awareness.

There are two parts to this week's exercise. First, to help you discern your level of awareness of God's presence and activity, we'll follow an ancient prayer practice, *examen* of consciousness. Here you'll ask, how aware am I of God's presence in the moment to moment? Second, you'll want to evaluate your ability to notice the state of your own soul. How is it with your soul? What are your current soul inclinations, needs, and longings? To help you discern the "state of your soul," we'll practice *examen* of conscience. Finally, you'll want to consider another aspect of your rule of life. Which particular practices might help you cultivate attentiveness?

Questions for Reflection and Discussion

1. **Reflect on the Word**

   Read Psalm 139 and note some of the ways in which God knows and attends to each of us.

2. **Reflect on our world**

   Which aspects of the predominant culture hinder attentiveness? Which aspects of the prevailing culture encourage attentiveness?

3. **Reflect on your spiritual journey**

   Think of a specific time when you sought and clearly discerned God's guidance or direction. In what ways did God reveal his direction and will (e.g., wise counsel, scriptures, circumstances, or prayer)?

4. **Reflect on your rule of life**

   Which spiritual disciplines will you practice to develop attentiveness to God's presence and activity in your life?

Examples:

1) In the near term (the next three or four months), I will practice daily *examen* of consciousness (instructions following).

2) I will meet once monthly with a friend, pastor, or spiritual
director for conversation about my spiritual life (see Spiritual
Discipline 8: Spiritual Friendship).

Which spiritual disciplines will you practice to develop awareness
of your soul?

Examples:

1) I will practice daily *examen* of conscience (following).
2) I will share on a weekly basis with my spouse or spiritual
friend how it is with my soul.
3) Once a week I will journal my thoughts on how it is with
my soul.

5. This week, complete Spiritual Discipline 3: Daily Examen.

Spiritual Discipline 3:
The Prayer of *Examen*

Search me, O God, and know my heart;
Try me and know my anxious thoughts;
And see if there be any hurtful way in me, And lead
me in the everlasting way.

PSALM 139:23–24

Almighty God, to you all hearts are open, all desires
known, and from you no secrets are hid: Cleanse the
thoughts of our hearts by the inspiration of your Holy
Spirit, that we may perfectly love you, and worthily
magnify your holy Name; through Christ our Lord. Amen.

THE BOOK OF COMMON PRAYER

Self-examination is not an invitation to psychoanalysis,
problem solving, self-lecturing, or ego-absorption. The
whole point of self-examination is to become more
God-centered by observing the moments when we
are or are not so.

MARJORIE THOMPSON

The Spiritual Exercises, or prayer of *examen*, originated with Ignatius of
Loyola, founder of the Society of Jesus, or Jesuits. In 1491, Ignacio de
Loyola was born into a family of nobility in northern Spain. While fighting
with the Spanish army he suffered a serious leg injury. During a prolonged
and difficult period of recovery, he meditated on the life of Christ in the

scriptures and pored over devotional classics such as *The Imitation of Christ* by Thomas à Kempis. Deeply moved to the point of conversion, he devoted his life to zealously serving Christ and his church. He made pilgrimage to the Holy Land and studied for years for the priesthood. Over time Ignatius wrote and revised the *Exercises*, a series of reflections, prayers, and practices designed for completion in a four-week retreat under the guidance of a spiritual director. He emphasized examining one's life in light of the life, death, and resurrection of Jesus.

Over the history of the church, people have practiced many variations of the prayer of *examen*. We'll approach the practice very simply here, focusing on two aspects of self-examination: *examen* of consciousness and *examen* of conscience. The Latin *examen* refers to the "tongue" or weight indicator on a balance scale, conveying the idea of "an accurate measure of the true situation."[14] We practice *examen* for the purpose of seeing two closely related spiritual realities—God's presence in our life and our response to his presence.

Awareness of God: *Examen* of Consciousness

In the first movement, the *examen* of consciousness, we prayerfully reflect on the happenings of our day to notice or discern God's presence or activity. "The *examen* of consciousness is the means God uses to make us more aware of our surroundings. . . . God wants us to be present where we are. He invites us to see and hear what is around us and, through it all, to discern the footprints of the Holy."[15] Regularly practicing *examen* of consciousness fosters our ability to notice the ways in which God is at work in our life. Sometimes God's presence is subtle, barely noticeable, like a whisper or passing thought. Other times we may notice his presence in the words of a particular scripture passage, the actions of a friend, or a dramatic shift in circumstances. The practice of *examen* helps us hone our ability to pay attention, to notice the ways God tends to speak and to move in our life. This noticing leads to the second movement of the exercise, noticing our response to God's presence.

Awareness of Self: *Examen* of Conscience

In the second movement, *examen* of conscience, we reflect back over a period of time (such as a day) and notice how we responded to the Spirit's leadings and promptings. Like David in Psalm 139:23–24 (above), in trust we invite God to search our heart. We recognize with gratitude those times when, by the grace of God, we responded to the Spirit's promptings. We ask God to show us those instances where we fell short of the virtue and likeness of our Lord. We acknowledge and name any shortcomings or failings that surface.

The *examen* of conscience involves three interrelated aspects—noticing, naming, and confessing. First, we ask God to help us discern or notice those areas where we fell short of Christ's character, in thought, word or deed. This could either be a sin of omission (not doing what we should have done) or a sin of commission (doing what we should not have done). Second, we name our specific shortcoming, asking God to help us discern the motivations or inclinations underneath the behavior. Finally, we acknowledge our specific shortcoming, bringing it to God in a prayer of confession.[16] We ask God to transform that area of our life by grace, to create in us a clean heart and renew a steadfast spirit within us (Ps. 51:10). As we confess our sins, we rest in God's faithfulness to forgive us and cleanse us of all unrighteousness (1 John 1:9).

Practicing the prayer of *examen*: Several evenings this week, set aside a brief time to practice this discipline. First, think back through your day and ask yourself, where did I notice God's presence and activity today (*examen* of consciousness)? Write your thoughts in a journal or discuss with a spiritual friend what you notice about your day.

Second, set aside a brief time to practice *examen* of conscience. Ask yourself, where did I respond to the promptings or leadings of his Spirit? Where did I not? How was I present to God and others in my day? How is the Spirit prompting me to do things differently? If it helps, you might pray through Psalm 51 or 139 and ask God to bring to mind any way that you fell short in thought, word, and deed. Or you might pray through the beautiful "Collect for Purity" from *The Book of Common Prayer* at the beginning of this exercise. Be prepared to share your experience of these practices and pray with your Thrive Group.

Notes

1. W.F. Arndt and F.W. Gingrich, *A Greek-English Lexicon of the New Testament and Other Early Christian Literature* (Chicago: University of Chicago, 1957), 505.

2. Dallas Willard, *Renovation of the Heart* (Colorado Springs: Nav Press, 2002), 18.

3. Francois Fenelon, *Spiritual Progress,* Christian Classics Ethereal Library; available at http://www.ccel.org/ccel/fenelon/progress.v.xvi.html.

4. See Dallas Willard's helpful discussion in *Renovation of the Heart* (Colorado Springs: Nav Press, 2002), 37.

5. Eugene Peterson, *The Contemplative Pastor* (Grand Rapids, MI: William B. Eerdmans, 1989), 4.

6. Ibid.

7. Theresa Ladrigan-Whelpley, "Benedict of Nursia: Rule," in *Christian Spirituality: The Classics*, ed. Arthur G. Holder (London: Routledge, 2009), 71.

8. Ibid.

9. Mikaela Conley, "ADHD on the Rise: Almost One in 10 Children Diagnosed, Says CDC;" available at http://abcnews.go.com/Health/adhd-cases-rise/story?id=14332873.

10 Shane Hipps, *Flickering Pixels* (Grand Rapids: Zondervan, 2009), 25.

11. Ibid., 78.

12. Ibid.

13. Ibid.

14.Richard J. Foster, *Prayer: Finding the Heart's True Home* (San Francisco: HarperCollins, 1992), 27.

15. Foster, *Prayer*, 28.

16. Ruth Haley Barton, *Sacred Rhythms* (Downer's Grove: IVP, 2006), 101–102.

CHAPTER 4

Prayer as Priority

We believe that the divine presence is everywhere and that in every place the eyes of the Lord are watching. . . . But beyond the least doubt we should believe this to be especially true when we celebrate the divine office.

BENEDICT OF NURSIA

All things must be done properly and in an orderly manner.

1 CORINTHIANS 14:40

Benedictine communities give priority to corporate prayer as the ordering rhythm of their days. Their days order around the divine office or *Opus Dei*, eight times of daily communal prayer. Benedict derives this rhythm from two verses in the psalms: "Seven times a day I will praise you," and "At midnight I arose to give you praise" (Ps. 119:62, 164). The divine office includes reading or chanting psalms, prayers, and other scriptures. According to their liturgy, or order of service, every week the community prays together through the whole Psalter. Over the days, weeks, and years, this predominant rhythm of prayer profoundly shapes the community. "It seeps into your bones," the abbot of a contemporary Benedictine community once remarked.

Eight times a day the monks leave their work, study, or other activities to corporately incline their hearts toward God. All other activities or concerns fall into place behind the priority of corporate prayer. The community considers the divine office or *Opus Dei* to be their "chief work." They approach their daily prayers with humility, devotion, and reverence. "Whenever we ask some favor of a powerful man, we do it humbly and respectfully, for fear of presumption. How much more important, then, to lay our petitions before the Lord God of all things with the utmost humility and sincere devotion" (*RB* 20). Although in later years some practices of fixed-hour prayer have become lengthy and elaborate, Benedict advises brevity in our corporate prayer. "We must know that God regards our purity of heart and tears of compunction, not our many words" (*RB* 20).

Benedict believes God is especially present in corporate prayer and urges sincerity. "Let us consider, then, how we ought to behave in the presence of God and his angels, and let us stand to sing the psalms in such a way that our minds are in harmony with our voices" (*RB* 19). Augustine advises similarly in the *Praeceptum*, "When you pray to God in psalms and hymns (Col. 3:16), meditate in the heart on what is expressed with the voice" (*Pr* 2:3). Both Benedict and Augustine implore us to align our hearts with the prayers of our lips.

Benedict recommends that the first period of prayer begin with *Vigils* or the Night Office at about 2 a.m. The Day Office begins with the second period of prayer at sunrise (first called *Matins*, now called *Lauds* for recitation of praise psalms). Monks recite *Prime, Terce, Sext,* and *None* at about 6 a.m., 9 a.m., noon, and 3 p.m. respectively. *Vespers* ends at sunset, and *Compline* ends the Day Office as darkness falls.[1] Additionally, Benedict recommends that the oratory or sanctuary of the monastery be set aside at other times for individuals wishing to pray privately (*RB* 52).

The Related Theme of Order

The practice of fixed-hour prayer exemplifies the monastic theme of order. Benedict outlines the liturgy of corporate prayer in great detail in his *Rule*, devoting sixteen of the seventy-three chapters to aspects of the divine office.

In these chapters he specifies not only the schedule for the prayer services, but the content—the specific scriptures, hymns, and prayers, with seasonal variations, and instructions for worship leaders and participants.

In addition to these hourly and daily rhythms (ordered by sunrise and sunset), a monastic community lives by the broader rhythms of the week, the seasons (a winter and a summer order), and the church year (the liturgical calendar). Along with the larger church, monastic community lives by the familiar rhythms of Jesus' life, as seen in the feast and fasts of the church year: Advent, Christmas, Epiphany, Lent, Easter, Pentecost, and so on.

This predominant rhythm of life, ordered around the life of Christ, is profoundly formative. "Liturgy gathers the holy community as it reads the Holy Scriptures into the sweeping tidal rhythms of the church year in which the story of Jesus and the Christian makes its rounds century after century, the large and easy interior rhythms of a year that moves from birth, life, death, resurrection, on to spirit, obedience, faith, and blessing."[2] If we allow them, year after year these greater shared rhythms begin to mold us together in corporate likeness to Christ.

Thus, on a larger scale, the life of a monastic community orders around what matters most—God's great redemptive story in which we all play a part. Beyond the walls of the monastery, Eugene Peterson makes a case for all Christ-followers to live by the church's liturgical calendar. Without a sense of God's greater story of redemption and our own part in it, we can all too easily get caught up in lesser pursuits. "Without liturgy we lose the rhythms and end up tangled in the jerky, ill-timed, and insensitive interruptions of public-relations campaigns, school openings and closings, sales days, tax deadlines, inventories, and elections."[3] We sometimes get lost in the smaller things of life and lose sight of the greater story that God is writing. With this in mind, monastic communities live with intentionality and purpose, allowing the broad movements of God's story to shape and order their lives, both as individuals and communities.

We've discussed the ordering of monastic time by fixed hours of prayer, but order characterizes additional aspects of monastic life.

Monks display a clear order in their community and an expected order or propriety in their conduct. First, a Benedictine community evidences a clear social ordering—a hierarchical ordering of persons within their community. One's rank is determined by the date of entry into the monastery, the character of the individual, and the abbot's discretion. With a keen sense of Christ's image in each of us, every person holds great value. Each holds a distinct place and fulfills clearly prescribed duties within the community. Second, an expected order or propriety governs their behavior. Throughout his *Rule*, Benedict uses consistent language to describe monastic behavior—all should be reasonable, dignified, and appropriate, with decorum, and restraint.

A contemporary reader might bristle at the prescribed order of the *Opus Dei*, the structure of the broader community or expectations for individual propriety. But in Chapter 18: "The Order of the Psalmody," we see the humility with which Benedict offers his various instructions. "Above all else we urge that if anyone finds this distribution of the psalms unsatisfactory, he should arrange whatever he judges better" (*RB* 18). Clearly Benedict does not prescribe these things with a heavy hand.

For the 6th century reader it is more likely that, given the extreme social, political, and economic upheaval of their time, the structure and order of the monastic community provided a welcome "haven of order" amidst the chaos. Monasteries offered a stable, predictable, and higher way of life in a notably chaotic and uncertain period. The rhythm of fixed-hour prayer held it all together, as the community regularly turned their attention to the person and presence of God.

Today within the greater church there seems to be a fresh interest in historic liturgies, rhythms, and practices. Perhaps in some way we find ourselves craving a similar "order amidst the chaos." As we follow these ancient ways, it roots us in the life of the greater church, spanning time and space. Order and rhythms offer a glimpse beyond the smallness of our individual lives into the grander scale of God's story and the people who follow him, the church universal.

Corporate Rhythms in Jewish and Christian Community

In the scriptures, corporate rhythms order and define the lives of both Jewish and Christian communities. In the life of ancient Israel, we find corporate rhythms of worship, prayer, and sacrifice. Scholars' opinions vary, but it appears customary to pray two to three times daily.[4] Over the years the frequency of daily prayer may have varied. For example, David writes, "Evening and morning and at noon, I will complain and murmur, and He will hear my voice" (Ps. 55:17). In violation of the Babylonian king's edict and at great risk to himself, Daniel continues his custom of praying three times a day (Dan. 6:10). Or, as mentioned above, Psalm 119 mentions praying seven times a day and at midnight (Ps. 119:164, 62). It's unclear whether this is meant literally or figuratively (seven seen as the number of completion). Whatever their daily rhythm or practice, the Sabbath orders their weekly rhythm (Ex. 20:8–11). Their years revolve around various feasts, fasts, and observances (e.g., the Feasts of Passover, Weeks or Pentecost, Tabernacles, and the Day of Atonement) and the greater rhythms of a seventh-year Sabbatical and fiftieth-year Jubilee.

In the Bible these greater rhythms of prayer, worship, and sacrifice shape and define the Jewish community of which Jesus was a part. And similar to the monastic hours of prayer observed centuries later, these corporate worship practices ordered their way of life. New Testament scholar Scot McKnight, in *Praying with the Church*, observes that the Jewish hours of prayer provided the ordering rhythm of their days. "Jews at the time of Jesus measure time in a variety of ways—none of them by a clock. There were morning prayers and late afternoon prayers and evening prayers, each of which was tied somehow to the worship of the temple. Time was not rooted simply in the economic system or in meal routines but more fundamentally by the temple's worship."[5] Over the years, this larger rhythm formed the community together as one.

In the Gospels, we observe Jesus engaging in both corporate and individual prayer. He participated in the corporate prayers and practices of the Jewish community (e.g., Passover), yet often withdrew to the wilderness to pray (Luke 5:16). In fact, we consistently find Jesus in solitude and prayer before significant events or demands. Before launching his earthly ministry, Jesus spent forty days in solitude in the wilderness (Matt. 4:1–11). Before choosing his twelve disciples Jesus prayed all night (Luke 6:12–13). Before the series of events leading to his crucifixion and resurrection, Jesus prayed fervently in the Garden of Gethsemane (Matt. 26:36–46).

At the same time, Scot McKnight makes the case that Jesus "reshaped the sacred rhythmical prayer practices of his world so that they would reflect his own kingdom mission."[6] In the Bible we see Jesus participating in the corporate practices of his people, while redeeming these practices to reflect his own purposes. When Jesus is asked how to pray, he offers the Lord's Prayer (Matt. 6:9–13). The Apostles continue his emphasis on prayer, instructing us to pray without ceasing (1 Thess. 5:17) and devote ourselves to prayer (Col. 4:2).

These deeply formative rhythms of corporate prayer and practice carry over into the early church. A passage such as Acts 2:42–47 offers a glimpse into the pattern of practices that shaped the lives of early Christ-followers. They devoted themselves to the apostles' teaching, fellowship, breaking of bread, and prayer. They held all things in common, selling their possessions and sharing with those in need. Daily "with one mind" they visited the temple, breaking bread from house to house, taking meals with gladness and sincerity, praising God, and having favor with all people. We find the Apostles observing the hours of prayer in Acts 3:1 (Peter and John go to the temple "at the ninth hour, the hour of prayer") and Acts 10:9 (Peter goes up on the housetop "about the sixth hour to pray").

We also find evidence of corporate prayer rhythms in the *Didache*, an early church document from the late first or early second century which distinguishes Christian belief and practice from Jewish and pagan belief and practice. The *Didache* instructs believers to pray the Lord's Prayer three times a day. Praying by set rhythms allows us to join our prayers with others in the worldwide church and habitually redirect our attentions and affections toward God.

The Priority of Prayer in Our Lives

Why is prayer a priority? As we've seen, at a corporate level prayer not only draws our hearts toward God, but draws us together as a praying and worshipping community to offer God's presence in the world. Prayer forms and shapes us as one people. In prayer, whether corporate or individual, we nurture and deepen our relationship with God. We set aside all else to be present to the God who is always present to us, to listen and respond to the voice of love. Prayer draws us nearer to God and nearer to one another.

Whether we pray corporately or individually, with set prayers or extemporaneously, at set hours or throughout the day, prayer demands priority because prayer turns our hearts away from our many things toward God. Prayer takes priority because these personal encounters with God transform us. "To pray is to change. Prayer is the central avenue God uses to transform us. If we are unwilling to change, we will abandon prayer as a noticeable characteristic of our lives. The closer we come to the heartbeat of God the more we see our need and the more we desire to be conformed to Christ."[7] Like Moses descending from the mountain with the glory of God shining on his face, when we spend time with God in prayer it shows in our lives. When we spend time with God in prayer, our lives will more and more reflect his glory.

Early 20th-century writer Evelyn Underhill reminds us of the significance of prayer in leading others in their faith relationship with Jesus Christ. The time we spend in prayer, in drawing our hearts near to God's, both forms us and informs our ministry to others. "What you are like, and what your relation to God is like; this must and will affect all those whom you visit, preach to, pray with, and to whom you give the sacraments. . . . And what you are like is going to depend on your secret life of prayer; on the steady orientation of your soul to the Reality of God."[8] Our character and our ministry to others depends on our relationship with God. We forge that relationship in prayer, as we come before God in search of his grace and help. Our "secret life of prayer" helps orient our souls, aligning our hearts more closely with God's.

A Different Relationship with Time

Again we find a theme—this different relationship with time, that benefits the contemporary reader. Prayer determines the rhythm in the monastery, not clocks, deadlines, mealtimes, or production goals. Dan Allender, in *Sabbath*, observes the dysfunctional relationship with time in contemporary culture. "We live in a time-troubled era. . . . Many people experience time as an unruly mess that is often out of control."[9]

We think of time in terms of needing it, making it, losing it, spending it, or using it like a commodity, writes Allender. Instead, he proposes, "time doesn't have to be redeemed or used or stolen or made or spent; instead, we are called to submit to time as the medium in which we live. Time is simply to be breathed as air."[10] One gets the sense that the monastic understands this way of life—not striving against or manipulating time, but submitting to it in the same way that he or she submits to God and his greater purposes in the world.

What kinds of priorities does contemporary culture tend to promote? Fattening our retirement accounts? Looking younger? Collecting followers or fans? Getting what we think we're "entitled" to? As followers of Jesus Christ, our priorities should be dramatically different. As we've seen, monastic communities prioritize corporate prayer. It serves as a predominate rhythm that orders and shapes their days, and ultimately the community itself. "This deep Church tradition of the hours of prayer, if one begins to live within its sacred time rhythms, functions as a protest against the busyness of the world enthralled by work and money and the relentless pursuit of the time clock."[11]

Like the monastic community, we can submit our lives to rhythms of prayer—greater rhythms that celebrate God's character and works and acknowledge our utter dependence on him. This act of worship destroys the idols of busyness, work, and money. If we choose different priorities and practices from the world, then we'll be formed and shaped very differently from the world. Like the monastic community, our desire to be formed not like the world but like Christ should inform our priorities.

A More Life-Giving Way

In the last chapter we examined our ability to pay attention, both to God's presence in our daily life and our response to his presence. Now we'll consider our priorities. First, take time to honestly consider the priority of prayer in your daily life. Does prayer hold the prominence you desire? What forms of prayer do you find meaningful? What would you like for your prayer life to look like going forward? Second, take time to consider, what are three or four personal priorities for you right now? Which priorities will order your rule of life in the near term (next season, semester, or few months)? How will your daily life reflect these priorities?

Questions for Reflection and Discussion

1. **Reflect on the Word**
   What priorities do you find in the Lord's Prayer (Matt. 6:9–13)?

2. **Reflect on our world**
   What priorities does the broader culture promote? What elements appear to "order" time in the broader culture?

3. **Reflect on your spiritual journey**

Have you experienced fixed-hour prayer? What about corporate prayer or praying prayers written by others? What has that been like for you?

....

....

....

4. **Reflect on your rule of life**

What priority do you give prayer in your daily life? What forms of prayer do you find meaningful? What prayer rhythms do you already live by (e.g., praying with my spouse in the evenings)?

....

....

....

Which prayer practices would you like to include in your rule of life?

....

....

....

Examples:
1) My spouse and I will pray with our children in the evenings.
2) I will practice conversational prayer throughout the day, praying as needs arise.
3) I will pray a breath prayer as prompted (such as "Lord Jesus Christ have mercy on me a sinner").
4) I will pray before each daily appointment or meeting.

More broadly, what current priorities drive you? What priorities will order your rule of life in the near term?

How will your rule of life reflect your priorities?

5. **This week, complete Spiritual Discipline 4: Fixed-Hour Prayer.**

Spiritual Discipline 4
Fixed-Hour Prayer

Prayer is often represented as the great means of the
Christian life. But it is no mere means, it is the great end
of that life.

P.T. FORSYTHE

The Psalter is the great school of prayer.

DIETRICH BONHOEFFER

In this chapter we noted how corporate prayer rhythms order and enrich monastic life. We looked briefly at prayer habits characteristic of the Jewish community and the early church. Likewise, participating in corporate prayer rhythms is at the heart of the tradition of Anglicanism and other liturgical traditions. In compiling the *Book of Common Prayer* in the 16th century, Archbishop Thomas Cranmer drew from various sources including monastic liturgies. But with everyday Christ-followers in mind, Cranmer simplified the daily prayer rhythms from eight times of prayer to a more realistic three—morning, noon, and evening prayer.

In addition to worshipping weekly with a community of believers, many people find the *Book of Common Prayer* a rich resource for their personal or familial prayer rhythms. The *Book of Common Prayer* offers orders for Morning Prayer, Evening Prayer, Noonday Prayer, and Compline, as well as Daily Devotions for Individuals or Families. The Daily Office Lectionary prescribes specific scripture readings (daily appointed Psalms, Old Testament,

Gospel and New Testament readings) for each day of the church year. We can use these readings as a guide for personal prayer and reflection.

Practicing fixed-hour prayer: This week, choose an interval by which to pray at fixed times this week (such as morning and evening) either corporately or alone. You might opt to attend a weekday Morning Prayer service at a local church. Or, you might pray at home using the *Book of Common Prayer*,[12] pray extemporaneously, or a combination of both. You may choose to simply pray a one-line prayer, or breath prayer such as the ancient prayer, "Lord Jesus Christ, have mercy on me a sinner" at intervals throughout the day. You might choose to pray a familiar prayer like the Lord's Prayer alone, with a friend or coworkers, or as a family.

Ideally, choose a daily rhythm and try to practice it each day between now and your next Thrive group meeting. Be creative and use whatever helps or reminders that you need, such as a cell phone alarm or appointment book. The point of this exercise is to offer a sense of the ways daily prayer rhythms form and shape us. Experiment with some possibilities and prepare to share your experiences with your Thrive Group. What benefits did you see in abiding by a daily prayer rhythm? What obstacles did you encounter?

Notes

[1] Benedict of Nursia, *The Rule of Saint Benedict*, trans. Anthony C. Meisel and del Mastro (New York: Doubleday, 1975), 110.

[2] Peterson, *Eat This Book*, 74.

[3] Ibid.

[4] Geoffrey W. Bromiley, *Theological Dictionary of the New Testament* (Grand Rapids: William B. Eerdmans, 1985), 283.

[5] Scot McKnight, *Praying with the Church* (Brewster, MA: Paraclete Press, 2006), 37.

[6] Scot McKnight, 52.

[7] Foster, *Celebration*, 33.

[8] Evelyn Underhill, *Concerning the Inner Life* (New York: E.P. Dutton, 1926), 11.

9. Dan B. Allender, *Sabbath,* The Ancient Practices Series (Nashville, TN: Thomas Nelson, 2009), 50.

10. Ibid., 51.

11. McKnight, 104.

12. For some prayers listed by topic, see "Prayers and Thanksgivings," *The Book of Common Prayer,* (New York: Church Publishing Incorporated, 1979), 809–841.

CHAPTER 5

Worship as a Way of Life

The chief end of man is to glorify God and to enjoy Him forever.

Westminster Shorter Catechism

Therefore I urge you, brethren, by the mercies of God, to present your bodies a living and holy sacrifice, acceptable to God, which is your spiritual service of worship.

Romans 12:1

In the previous chapters we discussed the importance of paying attention to our relationship with God—fostering our awareness of God's presence in our daily lives through spiritual disciplines such as scripture meditation, silence and solitude, *examen*, or prayer. In monastic community, the practices of prayer and worship come together in the divine office. This rhythm of daily prayer reveals the heartbeat of *The Rule of St. Benedict*. This rhythm of daily prayer offers a corporate turning of heart toward worshipping God, what they see as their "chief end." But the Benedictine community views worship more broadly. Worship is more than a particular activity practiced at a prescribed time and place, it's an orientation. Benedictine community finds God in all aspects of life. Benedictine worship has its roots in an abiding sense of God's presence and involvement in all things, even the humble, ordinary, and mundane. With this understanding, we offer ourselves, the whole of our lives, in worshipful service to God (Rom. 12:1).

In other words, worship becomes not just an activity found in the monastic liturgy or prayer book, but a way of life. "In arranging a monastic community, Benedict tried to create an atmosphere where God's holy presence dominates and colors everything. . . . Anything that distracts from constant awareness of the holiness of God and his creation has no place in the life of the monk."[1] Benedictine life is designed to foster awareness that we live and do all things *coram deo*, in the presence of God. The community lives with a deep awareness of life's sacredness, whether they're praying, studying the Bible, laboring in the fields, scrubbing a floor, or welcoming a stranger. With a heart inclined toward God, all of life can be offered as our spiritual service of worship.

Monastic community is a *worshipping community.* A monastic community approaches every aspect of life with this single-minded devotion. The ordinary stuff of daily life becomes their many-colored way of worshipping God, sometimes in solitude, sometimes in community, sometimes in silence, sometimes in word, sometimes in action, sometimes in stillness. Worshipping God forms and shapes the community as one body, reflecting Christ's likeness.

Divine Priorities

We're created to worship and we're shaped by what we worship. Poet Ralph Waldo Emerson is credited with saying, "A person will worship something, have no doubt about that. . . . That which dominates our imaginations and our thoughts will determine our lives, and our character. Therefore, it behooves us to be careful what we worship, for what we are worshipping we are becoming."[2] These words, "what we are worshipping we are becoming," should give us pause. Where do we tend to focus our affections and attentions? God often warns against idolatry in the scriptures, or anything that consumes our hearts and minds, anything that becomes more important than following after the way of our Lord. God warns against such things because as worshipping creatures, we tend to take on the likeness of what we worship.

Fundamentally, we're created to worship God, and in worshipping him we become more and more like him. But our hearts stray. In his great work *The Confessions*, St. Augustine recounts his painful years of searching until he finally discovers God. For years he experiences a deep inner restlessness until God draws him near. With a heart of sincere worship, Augustine begins *The Confessions* with high praise for God. "You arouse us so that praising you may bring us joy, because you have made us and drawn us to yourself, and our heart is unquiet until it rests in you."[3]

Augustine personally experiences the emptiness of not knowing God. After doggedly seeking to satisfy his restlessness and coming up empty again and again, he discovers the One infinitely worthy of our praise. In worship we discover our calling as beings made in the image of God, made for relationship with God. In worship we discover the profound joy of doing what our Creator designed us to do.

Augustine discovers out of the pain of personal experience, that our heart cannot truly find rest until God becomes the subject of our worship. He cautions those who reject God in search of something else. "Woe betide the soul which supposes it will find something better if it forsakes you! Toss and turn as we may, now on our back, now side, now belly—our bed is hard at every point, for you alone are our rest."[4] God's intervention in Augustine's life brings a deep sense of gratitude. "But lo! Here you are; you rescue us from our wretched meanderings and establish us on your way; you console us and bid us, 'Run: I will carry you, I will lead you and I will bring you home.'"[5] Clearly, Augustine has suffered for his "wretched meanderings," but again and again he experiences God's grace and consolation. The God who is slow to anger, quick to forgive, and abounding in loving-kindness, draws and receives us again and again.

Too often we try, but we cannot divide our affections between God and another. Jesus admonishes those who take up outward motions of worship while their hearts are turned elsewhere (Matt. 15:8). He invites us to worship God alone (Matt. 4:10). This is the way of true joy. Jesus teaches that God seeks those who worship in spirit and in truth, who worship with sincerity of heart by the Spirit of God (John 4:23). As the monastic community shows us, worship brings an abiding sense of God's constant and holy presence, invoking a wholehearted response. Worship is a way of life.

The Overflow of Worship

Acts of service, loving deeds overflow from our adoration and delight in God. Our worship prompts our service. "The divine priority is worship first, service second," writes Richard Foster. "Service flows out of worship. Service as a substitute for worship is idolatry. Activity is the enemy of adoration."[6] In other words, worshipping God becomes the priority out of which our service flows. Worship is the heart from which we serve. And even our acts of service can become idolatry when we elevate them above worship.

Evelyn Underhill affirms the priority of worship in the life of the believer. "Man's first duty is adoration, and his second duty is awe; and only his third duty is service." She continues, "We observe then that two of the three things for which our souls were made are matters of attitude, or relation: adoration and awe. Unless these two are right, the last of the triad, service, won't be right."[7] As Augustine and others have discovered, we find true delight in worshipping God.

Minding the Sacred in a Secular Society

In *Ancient Future Worship*, author Robert Webber notes the stark contrast between contemporary cultural attitudes and this ancient mindfulness that all of life is sacred. He observes the dualism in our current culture which causes us to see our relationship with God and faith practices (such as prayer and worship) as the sacred part of life and everything else—recreation, work, and relationships as the secular part of life. "However, the ancient, biblical mindset sees the whole day and indeed all of life—work, fun, marriage, and relationships—as the realm of the sacred."[8] As we've seen, rather than falsely compartmentalizing life into sacred and secular, the monastic community lives with a continual sense of the holiness that God's presence brings to

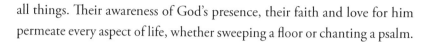

all things. Their awareness of God's presence, their faith and love for him permeate every aspect of life, whether sweeping a floor or chanting a psalm.

A More Life-Giving Way

In the last chapter you identified the priorities you'd like to live by, a handful of personal priorities which might shape or order your rule of life in the near term. Now we want to consider the place of worship. What place does worship hold in your life? What spiritual disciplines or daily practices might help you develop a deeper adoration, appreciation, or worship of God? What would it look like for worship to become a habit of heart for you? What might it look like for worship to become an ordering rhythm in your life? Sometimes we have neither the will or desire for what God calls us to. This week, as you consider the role of worship in your life, ask God to stir up in you a deeper desire to worship him.

Questions for Reflection and Discussion

1. **Reflect on the Word**
   Pray through a psalm of praise such as Psalm 103 and reflect on some of the reasons God is worthy of our worship.

   ....

   ....

   ....

2. **Reflect on our world**
   What idols do you see in the predominant or broader culture? What idols do you see in the contemporary church?

   ....

   ....

   ....

3. Reflect on your spiritual journey
What part has worship played in your relationship with Jesus?

4. Reflect on your rule of life
What priority does worship hold in your life now?

In the near term, what part will worship play in your rule of life?

Examples:
1) I will offer each conversation and task of my daily work as an offering of worship.
2) I will attend to the little opportunities throughout my day to worship God.
3) I'll begin each day by praying through a psalm as a discipline of worship.

5. This week, complete Spiritual Discipline 5: Worship.

Spiritual Discipline 5
Worship

Worship the LORD in the beauty of holiness.

PSALM 29:2, KJV

Then I looked, and I heard the voice of many angels around the throne and the living creatures and the elders; and the number of them was myriads of myriads, and thousands of thousands, saying with a loud voice, "Worthy is the Lamb that was slain to receive power and riches and wisdom and might and honor and glory and blessing." And every created thing which is in heaven and on the earth and under the earth and on the sea, and all things in them, I heard saying, "To Him who sits on the throne, and to the Lamb, be blessing and honor and glory and dominion forever and ever." And the four living creatures kept saying, "Amen." And the elders fell down and worshiped.

REVELATION 5:11–14

May the living God, who is the portion and rest of the saints, make these our carnal minds so spiritual, and our earthly hearts so heavenly, that loving Him and delighting in Him may be the work of our lives.

RICHARD BAXTER

In this chapter we discussed the ways members of the monastic community view all of life as their "spiritual service of worship" (Rom. 12:1), their joy and delight. The monastic community approaches all things with the understanding that we live and do all things *coram deo*, in the presence of God. The *Westminster Shorter Catechism* affirms that the chief end of man is "to glorify God and to enjoy Him forever."

Practicing worship: This week, let the first thought or action of your day be one of worship—an offering of yourself as your spiritual service of worship. Do this in whatever form you will, but make it your daily offering to God. For example, you might begin your prayer time each morning with adoration, expressing to God the ways in which you delight in his character or works. Or, you might go for a walk at sunrise and enjoy the beauty of creation. Or, your offering of daily worship may begin with getting your three kids dressed, fed, and out the door with lunches packed, all with an eye toward God as your "spiritual service of worship." Be prepared to discuss your experience with your Thrive Group.

How did beginning your day with worship impact the rest of your day? Describe your experience of approaching daily life with an ongoing heart of worship.

Notes

[1] Terrence Kardong, *The Benedictines* (Wilmington: Michael Glazer, Inc., 1988), 84.

[2] Ralph Waldo Emerson, as adapted by Chaim Stern, *Gates of Understanding*, (New York: Central Conference of American Rabbis, 1977), 216.

[3] Augustine of Hippo, *The Confessions,* Vintage Spiritual Classics (New York: Vintage, 1998), 3.

[4] Ibid., 119.

[5] Ibid.

[6] Foster, *Celebration*, 161.

[7] *Underhill*, 18.

[8] Robert Webber, *Ancient Future Worship: Proclaiming and Enacting God's Narrative* (Grand Rapids: Baker Books, 2008), 125.

CHAPTER 6

A Rhythm of Contemplation and Action

> The apostles gathered around Jesus and reported to him all they had done and taught. Then, because so many people were coming and going that they did not even have a chance to eat, he said to them, "Come with me by yourselves to a quiet place and get some rest."
>
> MARK 6:30–31

Thus far we've examined some life-giving aspects of the Benedictine way, fidelity to Christ, attending to our relationship with him, prayer as priority, and worship as a way of life. Another predominant theme in monastic life relates to the greater life rhythm by which the community abides. In our discussion we've already touched on the fact that corporate prayer orders their daily life. Here I'd like to illustrate how this fits into the larger scheme of the Christian life. In monastic community a distinct and soul-shaping pattern of practices makes up their days—prayer and work. In a broader sense, this rhythm can be thought of in terms of contemplation and action.

A devout follower of Benedictine rule, St. Gregory the Great (540–604), seizes on the idea of finding an appropriate rhythm of contemplation and action for his life. In *The Book of Pastoral Rule*, a kind of rule of life for pastors, St. Gregory advises that the pastor "should not reduce his attention to the internal life because of external occupations, nor should he relinquish his care for external matters because of his anxiety for the internal life."[1] Contemplation and action reveal complementary aspects of the Christian life. Typically, we're inclined toward one more than the other. Some of us find ourselves more naturally inclined to action while others of us are more inclined toward contemplation. According to Gregory, we should neglect neither. "Otherwise, he will either ruin his meditation because he is occupied by external concerns or else he will not give to his neighbors what he owes to them because he has devoted himself to the inner life only."[2]

Finding a rhythm of contemplation and action can prove challenging, but both offer integral aspects of Christian life. As we will see, the Christian life contains a number of reciprocities such as prayer and work, contemplation and action, solitude and community, giving and receiving. Each pairing acts as two sides of the same coin. To each there is a season. The monastic community seems to understand the reciprocity of contemplation and action in their daily life—a life comprised of prayerful dependence and active offering.

The counter movements of contemplation and action offer different yet corresponding aspects of the Christian life. Some people see this spiritual dynamic in terms of breathing in and breathing out. Gerald Sittser, in *Water from a Deep Well*, describes the Christian life as a rhythm of prayer and work: "God calls his people to two principal duties—prayer and work. Prayer draws us to God; work sends us into the world. Prayer centers and quiets us; work energizes us. Prayer restores us to God; work allows us to participate in God's restoration of the world."[3] In Sittser's description the give and take, the synergy of prayer and work becomes more apparent. Like breathing in and breathing out, both prayer and work bring life. Prayer, or breathing in, draws us near to God to receive his grace. In our work, or breathing out, we find the delight of giving to others from what we've received. In our work we experience the delight of loving others as we ourselves have been loved by Christ.

But Sittser cautions, "Without work, prayer becomes rote, vacuous and irrelevant, an empty discipline that shows little evidence of a deep concern for the world. . . . On the other hand, work without prayer becomes an idol."⁴ In other words, prayer or words without corresponding action can become an exercise void of meaning. And work without prayer becomes idolatry when lacking dependence on God.

Rhythms in the Life of Christ

As 21st century believers, there's great value in understanding the spiritual life in terms of the correspondence of contemplation and action. Following Christ includes both the prayerful dependence of Mary, sitting attentively and receptively at Jesus' feet, and the active offering of Martha serving Jesus (Luke 10:38–42).

> Now as they were traveling along, He entered a village; and a woman named Martha welcomed him into her home. She had a sister called Mary, who was seated at the Lord's feet, listening to his word. But Martha was distracted with all her preparations; and she came up to him and said, "Lord, do you not care that my sister has left me to do all the serving alone? Then tell her to help me." But the Lord answered and said to her, "Martha, Martha, you are worried and bothered about so many things; but only one thing is necessary, for Mary has chosen the good part, which shall not be taken away from her."

Notice in this passage Jesus' response to Martha's distress. "Mary has chosen the good part." Perhaps rather than thinking in terms of one being better than the other, we should think in terms of priority. Both prayerful dependence and active offering lend complementary aspects to the Christian life. But prayerful dependence, nurturing our relationship with Christ, receiving his grace, both *precedes and undergirds* active offering.

The Gospel accounts reveal the rhythms and practices at the heart of Jesus' "with-God" life. We find an example in Jesus' interaction with his apostles, who've recently returned from a mission trip. "The apostles gathered around Jesus and reported to him all they had done and

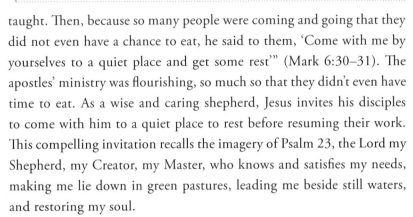

taught. Then, because so many people were coming and going that they did not even have a chance to eat, he said to them, 'Come with me by yourselves to a quiet place and get some rest'" (Mark 6:30–31). The apostles' ministry was flourishing, so much so that they didn't even have time to eat. As a wise and caring shepherd, Jesus invites his disciples to come with him to a quiet place to rest before resuming their work. This compelling invitation recalls the imagery of Psalm 23, the Lord my Shepherd, my Creator, my Master, who knows and satisfies my needs, making me lie down in green pastures, leading me beside still waters, and restoring my soul.

Here Jesus no doubt celebrates the apostles' good works but also recognizes their legitimate need for restoration before ministering further. God has hard-wired into us this limitation, this need for rest. Instead of fighting our limitations as we often do, Christ invites us to embrace them *as a gift*. Our Lord invites us to regularly lay down our work, to come away with him and rest. God renews and restores us through practices like prayer, worship, scripture meditation, spiritual friendship, and rest. As we step away from our work, God re-creates and restores our souls. And beyond our own need, having spent time with Jesus *we then have something to offer others*.

Jesus lives this rhythm of contemplation and action—withdrawing for life-giving solitude and prayer with the Father, then offering himself to others in ministry to their needs. Breathing in. Breathing out. Luke notes, "Yet the news about him spread all the more, so that crowds of people came to hear him and to be healed of their sicknesses. But Jesus often withdrew to lonely places and prayed" (Luke 5:15–16). In the face of great need, Jesus often withdraws to the wilderness and prays. Jesus' intimate relationship with the Father, fostered through prayer, becomes the priority upon which Jesus builds his life and ministry. As we live into a similar rhythm, we're embracing our God-given design. As we live into a similar rhythm, we're expressing our humble dependence and trust in God.

Our Desperate Need for Rest

In the Christian life, we tend to emphasize activity over prayerful dependence or contemplation. This is nothing new. In 1926, Evelyn Underhill cautions, "we are drifting toward a religion which consciously or unconsciously keeps its eyes on humanity rather than on Deity—which lays all the stress on service, and hardly any of the stress on awe: and that is a type of religion which in practice does not wear well."[5] We would do well to receive her advice today. Why doesn't this practice wear well? If we set our eyes on pleasing people instead of God, we'll quickly wear out. We keep our eyes on God for vital communion, renewal, and restoration. We keep our eyes on God to receive his direction and enablement to do the things he calls us to do. When we push ourselves beyond our limits, we suffer the spiritual consequences. Our life and ministry suffers. And because we're connected in community with other Christ-followers, the spiritual impact goes beyond us.

Finding Rhythms in a Culture Inclined to Arrhythmia

There's much for us to notice here. In the post-modern West we seem to suffer from a kind of *collective arrhythmia*. Somewhere along the way, as a society we've lost sight of the natural ebbs and flows of life—healthy rhythms of giving and receiving, work and rest, action and contemplation. Whereas in previous generations these rhythms formed around natural cycles of day and night, a weekly Sabbath rest or seasonal and agricultural rhythms such as planting and harvesting, our modern technologies allow us around-the-clock access to work and commerce. Our technologies provide us numerous advantages, but this 24/7, open-all-night kind of existence wears on our souls.

Richard Foster makes the sobering observation that "In contemporary society our Adversary majors in three things: noise, hurry, and crowds. If he can keep us engaged in 'muchness' and 'manyness' he will rest satisfied."[6] Noise, hurry, and crowds abound in contemporary culture, but Foster advises that to move beyond such societal realities, "we must be willing to go down into the recreating silences, into the inner world of contemplation."[7] Too easily we get caught up in the "muchness" and "manyness" around us and lose touch with our need for reflection, restoration, and rest. Too easily we get caught up in the pride of "doing things for God" rather than simply enjoying God. Too often, like Martha we find ourselves worried and bothered about so many things when only one thing is necessary—an abiding relationship with God nurtured through practices like prayer and adoration. Our acts of service to God and others become the fruit of that one necessary thing, our enduring and abiding fellowship with the triune God.

We cannot get around our need to regularly enter into these "recreating silences." We may avoid it for a time, but in doing so we distance ourselves from the one Person who truly renews and restores our souls. Eugene Peterson cautions strongly against busyness, remarking that the word *busy* is a symptom not of commitment but betrayal. He refers us to Hilary of Tours' characterization of busyness as a "blasphemous anxiety to do God's work for him."[8] "How can I lead people into the quiet place beside the still waters if I am in perpetual motion?" Peterson asks, "How can I persuade a person to live by faith and not by works if I have to juggle my schedule constantly to make everything fit into place?"[9]

In choosing rest instead of activity we're demonstrating trust. In choosing rest we're "letting go and letting God." We're acknowledging that God is God and we're not. Instead of trying to get around them, we're living into the limitations and needs of our God-given design.

A More Life-Giving Way

In the last chapter we looked at how our lives might become more worshipful. Now we want to look at the greater rhythms by which we live. In a few words, how would you honestly describe your rhythm of life right now? What metaphor would you choose? On the other hand, how would you like to live? What kinds of life rhythms would be truly life-giving for you? We described the rhythm of the Christian life as one of contemplation and action, or breathing in and breathing out. Are you more naturally inclined toward action or contemplation? How are you doing at contemplation—abiding in the soul-restoring presence of God on a daily basis? How are you doing at action—offering others the life and vitality you receive from Christ?

As always, I encourage you to consider these questions prayerfully. Ask God to reveal to you a rhythm of life which brings life to you and to those around you. Ask God to reveal to you a way that is both life-giving and God-honoring.

Questions for Reflection and Discussion

1. **Reflect on the Word**
   Read Mark 6:30–32. In what way does Jesus care for the disciples?

2. **Reflect on our world**
   What kinds of rhythms characterize the predominant culture?

3. **Reflect on your spiritual journey**
   As you look back at your Christian walk, are there any particular times or seasons when you struggled with finding a life-giving rhythm? What was it about that particular season that caused you

to struggle? Did you find yourself more inclined to contemplation or action?

4. **Reflect on your rule of life**

   How would you describe the rhythm of life that you now live? In what ways does it reflect the way in which you want to live as a Christ-follower? In what ways does it not?

   Breathing in: How do you want to incorporate *contemplation*, or soul-restorative practices in your rule of life?

   Breathing out: How do you want to incorporate *action* or offering to others the revitalizing life of Christ in your rule of life?

5. **This week, complete Spiritual Discipline 6: Rest.**

Spiritual Discipline 6
Rest

Most of us are more tired than we know at the soul level. We are teetering on the brink of dangerous exhaustion, and really cannot do anything else until we have gotten some rest.

RUTH HALEY BARTON

The LORD is my shepherd,
I shall not want.
He makes me lie down in green pastures;
He leads me beside quiet waters.
He restores my soul.

PSALM 23:1–3

Come to Me, all who are weary and heavy-laden, and I will give you rest. Take My yoke upon you and learn from Me, for I am gentle and humble in heart, and you will find rest for your souls. For My yoke is easy and My burden is light.

MATTHEW 11:28–30

Jesus sees our soul weariness and calls us to a different way of life. Jesus invites us to live life "yoked" with him—to follow his ways and rely on his abundant presence and power rather than our own limited resources. In Christ's day, a yoke was a heavy wooden harness used to tie oxen together. Their practice was to yoke a young ox with a stronger, experienced ox. Like the weaker ox tied with the strong, Jesus invites us to join with him. But rather than the heavy wooden harness of the oxen, Jesus' "yoke" is more like an embrace. Jesus invites us to an "easier" way, a way of life that he enables by his presence with us. Over time, following Christ by faith, depending on him for life and godliness, transforms our lives. The weary find rest for their souls. We exchange a burdensome life of independence for an easier life of dependence, of ongoing, soul-nourishing communion with Christ.

Taking time for regular rest expresses our dependence on Christ. In rest we offer ourselves to the Good Shepherd for needed restoration of body, mind and soul. In choosing to rest we recognize the God-given limitations of our human frame. We acknowledge that we are the created and not the Creator. We let go of the constant compulsion to produce, control and fix things. We cease our striving and doing and rest in God.

Practicing rest: We experience rest in many ways. In which practices do you find soul nourishment or soul rest? Perhaps you could spend a leisurely afternoon at a local art museum or arboretum, linger over a meal with friends, or engage in a favorite hobby. Maybe you first need to attend to your physical need for rest. Give yourself permission to sleep late one morning or nap in the afternoon. This week take time to get away with Jesus and get some rest. Be prepared to talk with your Thrive Group next week about your experience. How easy was it to disengage from your work for some "unproductive" time? What did it feel like to acknowledge and attend to your soul's need for rest?

Notes

[1] St. Gregory the Great, *The Book of Pastoral Rule*, trans. by George E. Demacopoulos (Crestwood, NJ: St.Vladimir's Seminary Press, 2007), 68.

[2] Ibid.

[3] Gerald Sittser, *Water from a Deep Well* (Downers Grove: InterVarsity, 2007), 114-115.

[4] Ibid.

[5] Underhill, 6-7.

[6] Foster, *Celebration*, 15.

[7] Ibid.

[8] Peterson, *Contemplative Pastor*, 17.

[9] Ibid., 19.

CHAPTER 7

Dying to Self and Living for Christ

And He died for all, so that they who live might no longer live for themselves, but for Him who died and rose again on their behalf.

2 CORINTHIANS 5:15

Renounce yourself in order to follow Christ...hate the urgings of the self-will.

BENEDICT OF NURSIA

Put on the new self, which in the likeness of God has been created in righteousness and holiness of the truth.

EPHESIANS 4:24

In the last chapter we looked at the greater rhythms of contemplation and action in the Christian life, as seen in the monastic rhythms of prayer and work. Now we turn our attentions to the way in which monastic communities live a self-giving or "cruciform" life—dying to self and living for Christ. At the beginning of his *Rule*, Benedict affirms, "This message of mine is for you, then, if you are ready to give up your own will, once and for all" (*RB* Prologue). Denying oneself is essential to following closely after Christ. In Benedict's view, we must "unquestionably conform to the saying of the Lord: 'I have come not to do my own will, but the will of him who sent me'" (*RB* 5).

Similar to Benedict, in *The Imitation of Christ*, Augustinian monk Thomas à Kempis challenges us to conform our whole life to Christ's. Spiritual progress depends "on complete surrender of your heart to the will of God, not seeking to have your own way in great matters or small."[1] Such total surrender or "death to self" is the way of discipleship. He urges us to deny ourselves and take up our cross daily (Luke 9:23–24). "Be assured of this, that you must live a dying life. And the more completely a man dies to self, the more he begins to live to God."[2] As Christ demonstrates, the great irony of the Christian life is that death to self proves to be the way of life with God. This way of life is radically different from prevailing cultural inclinations toward self-centeredness and self-absorption.

Many aspects of monastic life tie to this theme of dying to self and living for Christ—the virtues of humility, obedience, and self-discipline to name a few. Benedict urges us to exert every effort to deny ourselves and follow Christ, who enables our efforts: "Every time you begin a good work, you must pray to him most earnestly to bring it to perfection" (*RB* Prologue). Later in the chapter he affirms, "We must, then, prepare our hearts and bodies for the battle of holy obedience to his instructions. What is not possible to us by nature, let us ask the Lord to supply by the help of his grace." Benedict acknowledges the challenges of following Christ. He sees obedience as a "battle of holy obedience." And we look to God to supply the grace to obey him.

Costly Grace

"When Christ calls a man, he bids him come and die."[3] Such were the remarkable sentiments of 20th-century martyr Dietrich Bonhoeffer. In *The Cost of Discipleship* he writes, "To deny oneself is to be aware only of Christ and no more of self, to see only him who goes before and no more the road which is too hard for us. . . . All that self-denial can say is, 'He leads the way, keep close to him.'"[4] We must deny ourselves and follow closely after Christ, oblivious to the pain and hardship of our own suffering. How is this way of life possible? Bonhoeffer explains, we deny ourselves "by letting Christ alone reign in our hearts, by surrendering our wills completely to him, by living in fellowship with Jesus and by following him."[5] Out of love for Christ, enabled by the grace and power of his indwelling Spirit, in countless ways each day, both large and small, we lay ourselves down in obedience and surrender. Dying to self is both discipline and grace.

The simple truth is that following Christ costs something, something profound. Bonhoeffer refers to the true path of life as "costly grace." Following Christ is profoundly costly, yet it is grace because the way of the cross, death to self, leads to true life. Like the grain of wheat that must fall to the earth and die, "He who loves his life loses it, and he who hates his life in this world will keep it to life eternal" (John 12:25). In denying ourselves and following Christ we find fullness of life—the way of flourishing and well-being. The way without cost is the way of cheap grace—"grace without discipleship, grace without the cross, grace without Jesus Christ, living and incarnate."[6]

Living the Cruciform Life

What does it look like to live this way of the cross, this cruciform life? One way of characterizing such a life is *putting off Adam* and *putting on Christ*. The apostle Paul exhorts us to "lay aside the old self, which is being corrupted in accordance with the lusts of deceit . . . be renewed in the spirit of your mind, and put on the new self, which in the likeness of God has been created in righteousness and holiness of the truth" (Eph. 4:22–44). God's transforming grace in us enables a daily putting off of the old and putting on of the new—a daily dying to self and rising to new life. Bonhoeffer reminds us, "The source of the disciple's life lies exclusively in his fellowship with Jesus Christ. He possesses his righteousness only within that association, never outside it."[7]

As followers of Christ, we put aside vices such as anger, wrath, malice, slander, and abusive speech (Col. 3:8) and "put on" or cultivate virtues such as compassion, kindness, humility, gentleness, and patience (Col. 3:12). Beyond all of these things, we "put on love" (Col. 3:14). In Benedict and his followers, we find a deep desire to live a virtuous life in imitation of Christ. Benedict urges us to actively pursue virtues such as humility and obedience.

Putting off the old and putting on the new involves *repentance*—daily turning away from fleshly inclinations and increasingly offering more of our lives to God. Paul refers to this when he says "We who live are constantly being delivered over to death for Jesus' sake, so that the life of Jesus also may be manifested in our mortal flesh" (2 Cor. 4:10–11). Robert Webber calls this "living in the pattern of the death and resurrection of Jesus Christ."[8] With the enabling of God's Spirit, daily we endeavor to die to the urgings of the self and live in the newness of life we have in Christ. Webber calls repentance:

> A daily, even momentary, entering into the cross, bringing to the cross our rebellious self-centered turning away from God and his purposes for our life, so that all those ways in which we repeatedly fail to be what God has created us to be are nailed with him to the cross and carried to the grave, so that in union with him we might also continuously rise in the resurrection to the new life.[9]

Repentance is a daily, ongoing choice to bring more and more of our "old" self to death on Christ's cross so that we can experience more and more of his resurrection life.

Second, Christ invites us not only to repent or turn away from our own ways of doing things, but also to *continually respond* to his Spirit forming and shaping us in likeness to him. Personal growth is primarily about divine initiative and action, the working of God's Spirit in us, but Christ invites us to actively participate in and cooperate with God's gracious work in us. Puritan John Owen advises that "our whole lives must be spent in a course of diligent compliance with the progressive work of grace in us."[10]

Third, like the Benedictine community, we *imitate* Christ's life, imitation being both means and end of our spiritual formation. We imitate Christ's actions while recognizing the tension between the reality of the Spirit's formation of us into Christlikeness and the reality that we must "work hard and carefully at imitating Christ by adopting his lifestyle and patterns of life."[11] The gift of God's grace, the working of the Spirit within us, enables us to imitate Christ. Augustine recognizes that God's grace works through every aspect of our becoming like Christ, beginning with the desire to follow Christ. God "begins his influence by working in us that we may have the will, and he completes it by working with us when we have the will."[12] God works in us both to will and to work for his good pleasure (Phil. 2:13).

In sum, God's grace enables us to conform our lives to Christ's. Christ calls us to put off the old man and put on the new, to turn away from our own ways and bring more and more of ourselves to this grace relationship with God. He invites us to continually respond to God's transforming grace, to cooperate and participate in his will. We work hard to imitate or follow Christ—understanding that grace precedes, empowers, and accomplishes all good work.

Self-Denial in a Culture Inclined to Self-Absorption

At every turn these monastic themes seem to contrast the values of contemporary culture. Modern psychology, for example, "favors independence over dependence, confidence over feelings of inferiority, avoidance of pain, and a strong will. The *Rule* says just the opposite: submit to authority, feel your inferiority, embrace suffering, and have no will of your own."[13] The contrast should not come as a surprise since the monastic way is to imitate Christ, whose earthly life culminates in selfless sacrifice. Christ-followers operate from a very different set of values than the world. "Christ died," the Apostle Paul writes, "so that we who live might no longer live for ourselves, but for him who died and rose on our behalf" (2 Cor. 5:15).

In contrast to the monastic way, our predominant culture often breeds self-centeredness, self-absorption, and even narcissism. "If the culture does a thorough job on us—and it turns out to be mighty effective with most of us—we enter adulthood with the working assumption that whatever we need and want and feel forms the divine control center of our lives."[14] The monastic is well-aware of this human tendency toward self-interest. Discipline and striving are intended to work against these tendencies, although with a clear understanding that any progress is God's. Benedict advises, "Place your hope in God alone. If you notice something good in yourself, give credit to God, not to yourself, but be certain that the evil you commit is always your own and yours to acknowledge" (*RB* 4).

A More Life-Giving Way

In the last chapter we discussed the larger rhythm of prayer and work, or prayerful dependence and active offering, in the Christian life. We examined the rhythms we currently live by and considered how our life might reflect a healthy rhythm of contemplation and action. This week I invite you to prayerfully identify several specific ways you desire to grow in virtue of likeness to Christ in this next season of life. In what area is God inviting you to die to self and live for him? What will this look like in the next season? What specific practices or disciplines can reinforce these changes? Who can support your desire for life change?

Questions for Reflection and Discussion

1. **Reflect on the Word**
   Read Romans 6:1–13. According to the Apostle Paul, why were we buried with Christ through baptism into death (or crucified with him) (6:4, 6–7)? How are we to live this out (6:11–13)?

   ....

   ....

   ....

2. **Reflect on our world**

   Who or what does the predominant culture encourage us to live for? How is this promoted?

   ....
   ....
   ....

3. **Reflect on your spiritual journey**

   As you reflect back on your spiritual walk, think of one area of your life where you experienced transformation or growth in Christ. What process, people, or resources did God use to bring transformation or growth in your life?

   ....
   ....
   ....

4. **Reflect on your rule of life**

   What is one area in which you desire to grow in virtue or likeness to Christ? Or to put it another way, what is one way you believe God is calling you to die to self and live for Christ?

   ....
   ....
   ....

   What specific disciplines or practices could support this?

   ....
   ....
   ....

Examples:

1) This semester I will practice thirty minutes of silence at lunchtime each day.
2) For the next six weeks, I will accompany my friend to her chemotherapy treatments.
3) Once a week I will bring dinner to our elderly neighbor.

4) What kind of accountability or support would help? Who could provide accountability or support?

....

....

....

5. Complete Spiritual Discipline 7: Fasting.

Spiritual Discipline 7
Fasting

And after he had fasted forty days and forty nights, he then became hungry. And the tempter came and said to him, "If you are the Son of God, command that these stones become bread." But he answered and said, "It is written, 'Man shall not live on bread alone, but on every word that proceeds out of the mouth of God.'"

MATTHEW 4:2–4

My food is to do the will of him who sent me and to accomplish his work.

JOHN 4:34

But you, when you fast, anoint your head and wash your face so that your fasting will not be noticed by men, but by your Father who is in secret; and your Father who sees what is done in secret will reward you.

MATTHEW 6:17–18

In the Sermon on the Mount, Jesus offers the practices of giving, prayer, and fasting as normative aspects of life (Matt. 6:2, 5, 16). Unlike the practices of giving and prayer, fasting is a discipline of abstinence. In disciplines of abstinence, we set aside the fulfillment of a particular desire for a period of time to draw near to God.

The scriptures reveal that we practice the discipline of fasting, or other disciplines of abstinence, for various reasons. Often, fasting is associated with grief, a grievous response to sin or other dire or sacred moment. Scot McKnight defines fasting as "the natural, inevitable response of a person to a grievous sacred moment in life."[15] We see this in several biblical examples. First, during a three-week period of mourning, Daniel practices a partial fast that entails not eating any "tasty food," meat, or wine (Dan. 10:2–3). Similarly, fasting reflects Nehemiah's grief over the news that Jerusalem's walls lay in ruins. "When I heard these words, I sat down and wept and mourned for days; and I was fasting and praying before the God of heaven." (Neh. 1:4). Others fast in grief over sin (1 Sam. 7:6). Second, we can practice fasting for the purpose of discernment or preparation, such as when Jesus fasts for forty days and nights before beginning his earthly ministry (Matt. 4:2).

The discipline of fasting continued to play a role in the historic church. *The Didache*, an early church document of the late first or early second century, advises Christ-followers to fast twice weekly on Wednesdays and Fridays. The liturgical calendar which we follow today includes seasons of both feasting and fasting. The period of Lent (the forty-day period leading up to Easter) often includes fasting in some form in self-examination, repentance, and preparation for the celebration of Christ's resurrection from the dead.

The practice of fasting can help lessen the influence of various, even legitimate, desires in our life. In fact, Dallas Willard regards the seven deadly sins—pride, envy, anger, sloth, avarice, gluttony, and lasciviousness, as "legitimate desires gone wrong."[16] Akin to the Apostle Paul's advice to "discipline yourself for the purpose of godliness" (1 Tim. 4:7), Willard advises practicing disciplines of abstinence like fasting to "bring these basic desires into their proper coordination and subordination within the economy of life in his Kingdom."[17] We may fast or abstain where legitimate desires have become disordered. We fast or abstain to disengage or disentangle as the Spirit leads. We fast or abstain out of desire for God to place our lives in proper order or priority, from his perspective, according to the "economy of life in his Kingdom." In our increasingly "plugged in" existence, it may be particularly relevant to practice a periodic media or tech fast.

Practices of abstinence such as fasting can reveal the inclinations of our heart. Sometimes the only way to discern the importance of a particular habit or desire in our life is to deny its fulfillment for a period of time. "Fasting is an opportunity to lay down an appetite—an appetite for food, for media, for shopping. This act of self-denial may not seem huge—it's just a meal or a trip to the mall—but it brings us face to face with the hunger at the core of our being. . . . Through self-denial we begin to recognize what controls us."[18] In this sense, fasting can aid us in recognizing anything we may have allowed too much significance in our lives.

Finally, in the absence of food or other "props," we discover how truly rich we are in God. "Persons well used to fasting as a systematic practice will have a clear and constant sense of their resources in God."[19] We abstain from food to "feed" on Christ, recognizing as he does that bread alone does not sustain us, but "every word that proceeds out of the mouth of God" (Matt. 4:4).

I'd like to offer a word of caution here. Subduing the will or flesh is not as simple as denial and discipline. By grace, God can work through abstinence as a means of helping us detach from certain habits or inclinations, but it's not a simple cause and effect relationship. Like any spiritual discipline, we practice fasting as a humble offering to God. We might abstain from a normal or legitimate desire to pray, serve, or meditate on Scripture. But neither fasting nor any discipline offers the "formula" for a particular result. All disciplines depend on God's grace as the means of transformation.

Practicing fasting: In this chapter we discussed the Benedictine emphasis on dying to self and living for Christ. Christ invites us to daily lay aside the old self and put on our new self, "which in the likeness of God has been created in righteousness and holiness of the truth" (Eph. 4:22–24). This week use the practice of fasting as a means of laying aside a legitimate desire or habit and offer the absence of that practice to God as a means of drawing you near to him. For example, if you choose to fast from a meal, use any feelings of hunger as cues to pray or read the scriptures. You may choose to fast or abstain from some other practice or desire. Be prepared to share your experiences of fasting with your Thrive Group. In what ways was the practice of abstinence spiritually beneficial to you? In what ways was it difficult?

Notes

1. Thomas à Kempis, 128.

2. Ibid., 88.

3. Dietrich Bonhoeffer, *The Cost of Discipleship* (New York: Touchstone, 1995), 89.

4. Ibid.

5. Ibid., 164.

6. Ibid., 45.

7. Ibid., 183.

8. Robert E. Webber, *Ancient Future Evangelism* (Grand Rapids: Baker Books, 2003), 89.

9. Robert E. Webber, *The Divine Embrace*, (Grand Rapids: Baker Books, 2006), 148.

10. John Owen, *The Works of John Owen*, ed. William H. Goold, 24 vols. (1850–1855; Edinburgh: Banner of Truth Trust, 1965–1991), 3:405, as quoted in K. Kapic, "Evangelical Holiness," in *Life in the Spirit*, ed. J. Greenman and G. Kalantzis, (Downers Grove: InterVarsity, 2007) 114.

11. James C. Wilhoit, *Spiritual Formation as if the Church Mattered* (Grand Rapids: Baker Academic, 2008), 44.

12. Augustine, *On Grace and Free Will* 17.33, as quoted in Chan, *Spiritual Theology*, (Downers Grove: InterVarsity Press, 1999), 83.

13. Thomas Moore, Preface, in *The Rule of St. Benedict*, Vintage Spiritual Classics (Collegeville, MN: Vintage Books, 1998), xxi.

14. Peterson, *Eat This Book*, 32.

15. Scot McKnight, *Fasting* (Nashville: Thomas Nelson, 2009), xx.

16. Willard, *Spirit of the Disciplines*, 160.

17. Ibid., 160.

18. Adele Calhoun, *Spiritual Disciplines Handbook* (Downers Grove, IL: InterVarsity Press, 2005), 220.

19. Willard, *Spirit*, 167.

CHAPTER 8

A Community Known by Love

We love because He first loved us.

1 JOHN 4:19

By this all men will know that you are My disciples, if you have love for one another.

JOHN 13:35

Therefore be imitators of God, as beloved children; and walk in love, just as Christ also loved you, and gave Himself up for us, an offering and a sacrifice for God as a fragrant aroma.

EPHESIANS 5:1–2

Particularly in light of our highly individualistic American culture, we've emphasized that monastic rules are *communal* rather than individual. Monastic rules offer guidelines for life in sustained relationship with other believers. We find a similar prioritizing of community in the New Testament epistles. In the case of the Benedictine brothers or sisters who pledge stability upon entrance into the community, these relationships endure for a lifetime. Much effort goes toward working for the common rather than individual good. In the *Praeceptum*, Augustine suggests, "No one should work at anything for himself. All your work should be shared together with greater care and more ready eagerness than if you were doing things for yourself alone. For when it is written of love that it does not seek its own (1 Cor. 13:5), it means that it puts the common good before its own and not personal advantage before the common good" (*Pr* 5.2).

Although Benedict begins his monastic experiment as a solitary monk, ultimately he upholds the common life as the best means of spiritual formation. In community we have opportunity to imitate Christ, to walk in love as he did for us, to demonstrate virtues of charity, humility, forbearance, and self-denial. In community we have opportunity to offer ourselves as Christ, "an offering and sacrifice for God, a fragrant aroma" (Eph. 5:1–2). As his followers, Christ invites us to participate in the mutual self-giving and love of the Trinitarian community of Father, Son, and Spirit.

A monastic community, like a New Testament community, functions in both interdependence and mutual dependence on Christ. Monastic rules emphasize serving and supporting one another in growing in Christ's character as well as living in unity in their common pursuit. Their mutual dependence on Christ enables them to grow in his likeness, both individually and corporately. In a chapter entitled "The Good Zeal of Monks" (*RB* 72), we get a sense of how this looks from day to day. "Try to be the first to show respect to the other . . . supporting with the greatest patience one another's weaknesses of body or behavior . . . earnestly competing in obedience to one another." To fellow monks they must "show the pure love of brothers; to God, loving fear; to their abbot, unfeigned and humble love." These exhortations echo the "one another's" of the New Testament, exhortations to love and serve one another in imitation of Christ.

Benedict first admonishes us to offer respect to all people. Augustine writes similarly, "Therefore, you should all live united in mind and heart (Acts 4:32) and should in one another honor God, whose temples you have become" (*Pr* 1.8). We respect and value each other because each person is created in God's image and indwelt by his Spirit. We delight in Christ's likeness in one another, encouraging this likeness to flourish and grow.

Second, "with the greatest patience," we bear with one another in our many weaknesses and failings. This too echoes New Testament exhortations. "Now we who are strong ought to bear the weaknesses of those without strength and not just please ourselves. Each of us is to please his neighbor for his good, to his edification. For even Christ did not please Himself" (Rom. 15:1–3). With a healthy sense of our own failings, we follow Christ's example of forbearance and patience in the weakness and shortcomings of another, building each other up in love.

Benedict urges the community to demonstrate their charity in service. "The brothers should serve one another . . . for such service increases reward and fosters love" (*RB* 35). Benedict advises us to serve one another, extending special kindness to the frail, weak, or sick among us. "Let those who are not strong have help so that they may serve without distress, and let everyone receive help as the size of the community or local conditions warrant" (*RB* 35).

Both Augustine and Benedict's rules dismiss any talk of fairness or equality in the community. Mindful not to discourage, Benedict advises that weaker brothers be given lighter work appropriate to their ability. "Brothers who are sick or weak should be given a type of work or craft that will keep them busy without overwhelming them, or driving them away" (*RB* 48). With gratitude for the gift of health and strength, the stronger among them shoulder more of the burden and help their weaker brothers. All members contribute in some way, but even in their work they emphasize encouraging and building each other up (1 Thess. 5:11). When we encounter another's weakness of body, mind, or spirit, Benedict invites us to respond as Christ, with patience and grace. At the same time, we ought to encourage one another in holy living, keeping each other accountable. "We urge you, brethren, admonish the unruly, encourage the fainthearted, help the weak, be patient with everyone" (1 Thess. 5:14).

Third, Benedict exhorts us to "earnestly compete" in obedience to one another. He admonishes us to make every effort to obey Christ and follow him closely. Christ both sets the example and enables us to live such holy lives. We run with endurance the race set before us, fixing our eyes on Jesus, the author and perfecter of our faith (Heb. 12:1–2).

Fourth, Benedict admonishes us to love God and one another (Matt. 22:37–39). In very practical terms, Augustine offers an example of what love looks like in monastic community. "You should take care, then, not to use harsh words; but if they have escaped from your mouth, then do not be ashamed to let the mouth which caused the wound provide the cure" (*Pr* 6.2). Both Augustine and Benedict urge their communities to keep short accounts—to habitually offer and receive forgiveness with haste.

Throughout the *Rule*, Benedict provides detailed instructions for living the common life: from suitable clothing, to sleeping arrangements, to the proper amount of food and drink, care of the sick, appropriate responses to errant brothers, and the procedure for leaving the monastery on errand. In the day-to-day running of the house we see Benedict's moderation in comparison with other monastic rules. For example, while desert monks follow a harsh aesthetic, living on bread and water, Benedict allows several meals, cooked foods, fresh fruit and vegetables as well as a moderate amount of wine. Their daily schedule allows for enough sleep. He provides them with necessities including a bed with pillow and covering and adequate clothing. Benedict insists that each has what they need, but nothing excessive. "Necessary items are to be requested and given at the proper times, so that no one may be disquieted or distressed in the house of God" (*RB* 31). Always pastoral, Benedict sees no need to leverage his authority over others or cause undue distress by unnecessarily harsh treatment.

Care of Souls

The idea of caring for souls traces back to the earliest days of the church. Benedict's guidance on the care of souls proves particularly insightful, for Benedict excels in his pastoral insight and ability to care for those entrusted to him. In Benedict's eyes, the abbot serves as father, physician, and shepherd. He approaches his role as spiritual father with devotion and love. The abbot holds the place of Christ in the monastery and leads by example more than word (*RB* 2). Echoing the theme of working toward the common good, the abbot seeks profit for the monks, not preeminence for himself (*RB* 64).

> He must know what a difficult and demanding burden he has under-taken: directing souls and serving a variety of temperaments, coaxing, reproving, and encouraging them as appropriate. He must so accom-modate and adapt himself to each one's character and intelligence that he will not only keep the flock entrusted to his care from dwindling, but will rejoice in the increase of a good flock. . . . Rather, he should keep in mind that he has undertaken the care of souls for whom he must give an account (*RB* 2).

As his language reveals, Benedict understands the many challenges of directing souls, particularly the need to adjust one's care to various tem-peraments, levels of maturity, and intelligence. With love and forbearance, he accommodates and adapts himself to each one. A Benedictine abbot or abbess exercises his or her responsibility with humility, discernment, and moderation, tirelessly working for the good of those they serve.

> He must hate faults but love the brothers. When he must punish them, he should use prudence and avoid extremes; otherwise, by rubbing too hard to remove the rust, he may break the vessel. He is to distrust his own frailty and remember not to crush the bruised reed (Isa. 42:3). By this we do not mean that he should allow faults to flourish, but rather, he should prune them away with prudence and love as he sees best for each individual (*RB* 64).

This passage well articulates Benedict's approach to pastoral care—prudence and persistence out of love. Because of his love for the brothers, he must address their faults, not ignore or excuse them. But we find great wisdom and compassion in his way of addressing them. If he must discipline, he does so with prudence, avoiding excesses that would demoralize or discourage. His leadership should invoke their love, not fear. He leads with discernment, moderation, and careful consideration. Here is a picture of a wise and loving father, like the Father of Hebrews 12 who disciplines those he loves, "for our good, that we may share His holiness" (Heb. 12:10). In the spirit of God the Father, the abbot disciplines out of love, always for the sake of reform.

Responding to the Errant Brother

Beyond his roles as shepherd of souls and loving father, Benedict responds to wayward brothers with the wisdom and compassion of a doctor nursing the sick. He discretely calls upon mature brothers to aid in their restoration. In a chapter entitled "The Abbot's Concern for the Excommunicated" (*RB* 27), he advises:

> The abbot must exercise the utmost care and concern for wayward brothers, because it is not the healthy who need a physician, but the sick. Therefore, he ought to use every skill of a wise physician and send in *senpectae*, that is, mature and wise brothers who, under the cloak of secrecy, may support the wavering brother, urge him to be humble as a way of making satisfaction, and console him lest he be overwhelmed by excessive sorrow. Rather, as the Apostle also says: Let love for him be reaffirmed, and let all pray for him (*RB* 27).

With a deep desire not to lose any sheep entrusted to him, Benedict comes alongside a wayward brother with a great sense of care and urgency. He sends in mature brothers to console, support, and encourage their wavering brother. He invites them to reaffirm their love for the brother and pray for him. Benedict's compassionate language calls to mind Pauline passages like 2 Corinthians 2:7–8, "forgive and comfort him, otherwise such a one might be overwhelmed by excessive sorrow. . . . I urge you to reaffirm your love for him." Benedict's concern is to love and console the weaker brother, to urge him toward humility, and support him in repentance—disciplining for the sake of reform, and all with great discretion, "under the cloak of secrecy." Benedict understands his role as caring for the sick rather than "tyranny over the healthy."

The Correspondence of Community and Solitude

In *Life Together*, Dietrich Bonhoeffer writes about common life in the underground seminary he founded. As leader of this clandestine Christian fellowship he suggests that community and solitude offer integral and corresponding aspects of the common life. Like the complementary movements of contemplation and action, community and solitude form yet another correspondence in the Christian life. Bonhoeffer notes that in any Christian community we'll find two kinds of people. Some fear being alone and spend far too much time in the company of others. Others fear community and spend far too much time alone. Bonhoeffer cautions against both extremes. "Let him who cannot be alone beware of community. Let him who is not in community beware of being alone."[1]

In appropriate measure, community and solitude offer corresponding aspects of common life. Time in solitude with the Lord bears fruit when we gather with others. And time in fellowship with other Christ-followers bears fruit in our time alone. Bonhoeffer explains, "Each by itself has profound pitfalls and perils. One who wants fellowship without solitude plunges into the void of words and feelings, and one who seeks solitude without fellowship perishes in the abyss of vanity, self-infatuation, and despair."[2] If we are much in community without adequate time in solitude, we find little depth in our fellowship. On the other hand, much solitude without adequate time in community can incline us toward self-absorption.

The Building Up of the Body of Christ

As we've discussed, monastic community operates as an interdependent unity of persons, each person contributing to the common good. In the epistles we find a similar emphasis on unity and oneness in the Spirit, as well as loving and serving one another. All is done in mutual dependence on Christ. The Apostle Paul uses the metaphor of the human body to explain the interrelationship of believers in Christ. "We who are many are one body in Christ, and individually we are members who belong to one another" (Rom. 12:5).

By the same Spirit, God gives a variety of gifts and ministries. God gives these "for the common good" and he produces the fruit or results (1 Cor. 12:4–7). According to the grace given us, God gives gifts such as prophecy, service, teaching, exhortation, leadership, or mercy and invites us to use them for the building up of the church (Rom. 12:6–8). God gives spiritual gifts *for the sake of others*. In discerning a rule of life, it's important to discern how God invites us to offer our gifts. This week we'll take time to identify the gifts, abilities, and resources God has given us, and prayerfully consider how God invites us to offer them.

In the letter to the Ephesians, Paul emphasizes the growth of the body as a whole. God provides prophets, evangelists, pastors, and teachers to equip members of the community for ministry. God gives spiritual gifts to Christ's followers to build up the body of Christ so that we might grow together as a community, toward unity and maturity in him (Eph. 4:12–13). As each person contributes, we grow up in all aspects into Christ the head (Eph. 4:15–16). In this shared vision of growth, each individual contributes something unique and valuable.

How do we know our spiritual gifts? You can find a variety of free spiritual-gift inventories or tests online, but a better way to discern your gifting is through serving in a local church or ministry. Volunteer in a short-term capacity in several different areas. Ask several pastors, mentors, or spiritual friends for their feedback and observations. To discern gifting you might consider the following questions: What am I most passionate about contributing to the body of Christ? What do I consider the most pressing need in the church or the world today? Where have I seen my efforts bear fruit? What have other people, particularly those who know me well, affirmed in my ministry or service to others?

In addition to offering our spiritual gifts, we can offer God-given skills, abilities, and resources for the building up of the church. If you're a gifted artist, consider the many ways you might contribute in the church. One thinks of Bezalel, a craftsman who contributed to Israel's first tabernacle, gifted "with the Spirit of God in wisdom, in understanding, in knowledge, and in all kinds of craftsmanship" (Ex. 31:3). God gifts these artisans with skills and abilities used to create the sacred tabernacle, its beautiful furniture and objects.

Peter admonishes us to offer our God-given gifts to the glory of God. "As each one has received a special gift, employ it in serving one another as good stewards of the manifold grace of God" (1 Pet. 4:10). God invites us to faithfully steward the gifts he gives us, to use those gifts in service to one another. Peter continues, "Whoever speaks, is to do so as one who is speaking the utterances of God; whoever serves is to do so as one who is serving by the strength which God supplies; so that in all things God may be glorified through Jesus Christ" (1 Pet. 4:11). One of the great joys of the Christian life is employing our gifts, abilities, and resources for the building up of the church to the glory of God—giving back to God out of that which he has given us. We find deep fulfillment in following God's unique call on our life.

Finally, we want to consider how our individual life stories or experiences have uniquely prepared us for life and ministry. This is a big topic, but this week spend some time reflecting on your story in relation to your giftings. How might specific aspects of your life story inform your particular passions or interests? In what ways has your personal story influenced the way you desire to contribute to the body of Christ? As you think about it, what themes or patterns do you see in your story? For example, your desire to be a nurse in third-grade may not have led to a nursing career, but it may be an indication of a gift for nurture and care. How is God inviting you to steward well the story he is writing in your life? And as author Dan Allender suggests, how is God inviting you to coauthor your story? [3]

Deeply Connected in a Culture Inclined to Individualism

A clear picture of community emerges in these monastic rules, a picture we would do well to notice. In *Flickering Pixels*, Shane Hipps explores the ways our various technologies or tools shape and form us, both as individuals and as communities. He traces the impact of technology through history, dividing it into three broad time periods—oral culture (before the printing press), print culture, and the electronic age.

Hipps describes oral culture as tribal, deeply connected, and empathetic. The need for oral transmission of information necessitates close community and interdependent relationships. Benedict and the early monastics fall into this period. Second, the printing press ushers in the print culture, which Hipps characterizes as individual, distant, and detached. Hipps' concern here is the potential redefining of the church coming out of the print age. "The technology of printing has helped erode the communal nature of faith. Community in the print age has been understood primarily as a collection of discrete individuals working concurrently on their personal relationships with Jesus."[4] In some respects, the contemporary church seems to have lost sight of the oneness and interdependence of the body of Christ.

Finally, Hipps refers to the present period as the electronic age. If oral culture can be characterized as tribal and print culture as individual, then our idea of community in the current electronic age has become a "tribe of individuals."[5] Or to put it another way, "If oral culture is intensely connected or empathetic and print culture is distant or detached, then our electronic experience creates a kind of empathy at a distance."[6] Picture a group of individuals in a room. Rather than engaged in conversation, each one is turned to their personal tech device . . . physically present, but not together in any meaningful way. This perception of community as a "tribe of individuals" sharply contrasts the deep connectedness of monastic community (or New Testament community), with relationships of self-giving and mutual dependence on Christ.

A More Life-Giving Way

In the last chapter we identified several ways we desire to grow in virtue and likeness to Christ in this next season. Now we want to examine our own experiences of relationship or community, whether within your family, church, small group, or among spiritual friends. What qualities characterize these relationships or communities? Which relationships are significant to you right now? Perhaps one priority of your rule will be to identify how you can attend to these relationships. How can you better embody the self-giving spirit we've talked about here? Second, you'll want to identify any spiritual gifts, skills, abilities, or resources you can offer. Third, consider how specific aspects of your life story might inform or direct your service in the church. In what ways have your experiences or life journey influenced the way you might contribute to the body of Christ? What are some ways you might offer your gifts? For guidance on identifying spiritual gifts, see Romans 12, 1 Corinthians 12, and Ephesians 4.

Questions for Reflection and Discussion

1. **Reflect on the Word**
   Read 1 Thessalonians 5:11–22 or Romans 12:9–21. List characteristics of Christian community.

2. **Reflect on our world**
   How does the predominant culture define love? Compare and contrast this with the Christian understanding of love.

3. **Reflect on your spiritual journey**

   As you look back at your Christian walk, in what ways have you experienced the kind of loving, supportive community we see in New Testament or monastic communities? What was that like?

4. **Reflect on your rule of life**

   Make a list of the significant people in your life right now (family, friends, colleagues, those with whom you worship or serve).

   How can you better attend to these relationships?

   List the corporate or shared rhythms and practices at your church.

   Consider any shared practices that are part of your regular family rhythms. What are some spiritual disciplines or regular rhythms which you would like to practice with your family?

Examples:

1) Next month I'll read through the book of 1 Timothy at lunch with several coworkers.

2) My spouse and I will share a simple Sunday dinner each week, inviting friends and family as we're able.

3) This summer we'll participate in a family mission trip.

What spiritual gifts has God given you? What other abilities and resources has God given you?

In what ways is God inviting you to offer your gifts, abilities, resources, or experience in service to the church?

5. **Complete Spiritual Discipline 8: Spiritual Friendship.**

Spiritual Discipline 8
Spiritual Friendship

No longer do I call you slaves, for the slave does not know what his master is doing; but I have called you friends, for all things that I have heard from My Father I have made known to you.

JOHN 15:14–15

If the bond of your mutual liking be charity, devotion and Christian perfection, God knows how very precious a friendship it is! Precious because it comes from God, because it tends to God, because God is the link that binds you, because it will last forever in him. Truly it is a blessed thing to love on earth as we hope to love in Heaven, and to begin that friendship here which is to endure forever there.

ST. FRANCIS OF SALES

What qualities do we find in spiritual friendship? In his book *Sacred Companions*, David Benner suggests that spiritual friends offer gifts of presence and hospitality. Spiritual friends offer hospitality by "making room" in our lives for others. We ask God to cultivate a "place" of quiet within us—the capacity to willingly receive and care deeply for others. Such inner hospitality is wrought out of abiding times in the presence of God. As we receive from the Lord, we develop the capacity to welcome and attend to others as he does.

Spiritual friends offer the gift of presence. "Presence begins with a still place within one's self. And, of course, I must learn to be still before

God if I am to learn to be still in myself." [7] In other words, if we desire to be a spiritual friend to another—to offer gifts of hospitality or presence, we must first learn to be present and still before God. We bring the fruits of our relationship with God into our friendships with others. Out of this inner stillness, or rootedness in God's presence, we offer gifts of hospitality, presence, and attentiveness.

Presence begins with careful attentiveness. A spiritual friend prayerfully attends both to the other person and to God's presence in that person's life. Spiritual friends help each other notice God's movement in their lives. To spiritual friendship we bring a genuine interest and delight in the other person and a sincere desire for their growth and flourishing in relationship with Christ. We accompany one another in the journey of spiritual formation, with an understanding that each soul is unique. We bring an appreciation for the other and attentiveness to what God might be doing in that person's life. The assumption is that God is at work. Our task as a spiritual friend is to help discern the movement of God in another's life.

Attentiveness to another person involves setting some things aside. "It usually means setting aside my own interests and preoccupations. It also demands that I stop analyzing what I am hearing or rehearsing how I will respond. . . . It also involves resisting the impulse to solve problems or fix things that appear broken." [8] In other words, to offer presence to another, we need to set aside the ways we often tend to engage with others.

In spiritual friendship we lay aside our inclinations to solve problems, advise, or fix the other person. At some point there may be a place to offer counsel or shared experience, but initially the emphasis is on simply offering our presence and listening attentively. The emphasis is on together attending to each person's experiences of God, their longings for him, their progress in living the spiritual life, and their practice of various spiritual disciplines such as prayer and worship. Spiritual friends support one another in prayer and help each other respond to God. In a spiritual friendship we humbly offer the presence of Christ in us because the presence of Christ brings transformation. "As I bring my true self-in-Christ to relationships of spiritual friendship, what the other person encounters is not just me but Christ in me."[9]

Finally, spiritual friends bring their true or authentic self to the relationship—the brokenness, questions, tensions, hopes, and prayers of our daily lives. Spiritual friendship offers a place for both giving and receiving, for knowing and being known, for shared encounter of the joys and challenges of the spiritual life. Like our Lord, spiritual friends offer grace and truth. Teresa of Avila writes of the gracious truthfulness that characterizes spiritual friendship. "I wish that we five, who now love each other in Christ . . . might arrange to come together now and then in order to dispel one another's illusions and to advise one another of ways in which we could improve ourselves and be more pleasing to God. For no one knows himself so well as those who observe him, provided they do so lovingly and with the wish to do him good."[10] A relationship of spiritual friendship provides a safe and nurturing context for addressing those areas where we desire to grow in virtue and likeness to Christ, a way in which we can faithfully accompany each other on the spiritual journey.

Practicing spiritual friendship: This week, schedule some time for a leisurely coffee or meal with a close spiritual friend. Take time to simply share with each other what your spiritual journey has been like lately and how it is with your soul. Consult the list below for several topics of conversation. Notice your own capacity for hospitality, presence, and attentiveness. Perhaps a weekly conversation with this particular spiritual friend can become an aspect of your rhythm of life. Be prepared to share your experience with your Thrive Group.

Questions spiritual friends might ask each other:

- How is it with your soul today?
- Where are you noticing God or experiencing his presence lately?
- How is God inviting you to respond to what you are noticing?

- What are you finding life-giving these days?
- What are you finding difficult, taxing, or draining?
- What are you longing for or needing?
- How can I pray for you?

Notes

[1.] Bonhoeffer, *Life Together,* 78.

[2.] Ibid.

[3.] If you're interested in reflecting more deeply on your life story, there are some great resources available. For example, see Dan Allender's *To Be Told: God Invites You to Coauthor Your Future,* (Colorado Springs: Waterbrook Press, 2005), or the Listen to My Life resources at www.onelifemaps.com.

[4.] Hipps, 57.

[5.] Ibid., 107.

[6.] Ibid., 108.

[7.] David G. Benner, *Sacred Companions* (Downers Grove, IL: IVP, 2002), 47.

[8.] Ibid., 50.

[9.] Ibid., 52.

[10.] Teresa of Avila as quoted in Richard Lamb, *The Pursuit of God in the Company of Friends* (Downers Grove: IVP, 2003), 178.

CHAPTER 9

Contemptus Mundi and Amor Mundi

He has told you, O man, what is good; And what does the Lord require of you but to do justice, to love kindness, And to walk humbly with your God?

MICAH 6:8

Pure and undefiled religion in the sight of our God and Father is this: to visit orphans and widows in their distress, and to keep oneself unstained by the world.

JAMES 1:27

Ultimately, when we touch the things of the world, the only question we need ask ourselves is, "How is this thing affecting my relationship with the Father?"

WATCHMAN NEE

In the previous chapter we discussed the nature of monastic community. Over the centuries, Benedict and others in Christian community committed to relationships of mutual love and self-giving. We discussed Paul's emphasis on the corporate growth of the body of Christ and considered ways God gifts each of us for the building up of the church. In this chapter, I'd like to discuss the relationship of the monastic community to the world. In referring to the world here, I'm not referring to the natural world which

God created. I'm referring to aspects of the surrounding culture (mankind's construct) that run counter to the ethic of God's kingdom, characterized by mercy, justice, and love (Mic. 6:8). As N.T. Wright suggests, I'm referring here to the world "as it places itself over and against God . . . the world as it is in rebellion against God: the world as the combination of things that draws us away from God."[1] With this in mind, a monastic community exists in dual relationship with the world. Their relationship with the world can be characterized by two ancient Latin phrases, *contemptus mundi* and *amor mundi.*

Contemptus mundi, or contempt for the world, refers to detachment from worldly ways of making life work. Quaker Thomas Kelly describes the relationship of the Christ-follower to the world as being "torn loose from all earthly attachments and ambitions."[2] Its counterpart, *amor mundi,* joins us to God in a deep compassion or concern for those caught up in worldly attachments and ambitions. Kelly refers to this orientation as our being "quickened to a divine but painful concern for the world."[3] In *contemptus mundi* and *amor mundi* we again find another correspondence of the Christian life. The monastic community, or any Christ-follower, relates to the world in both ways. God invites us to live in a distinctly different way from the world and also to actively join him in offering Christ's love and compassion to the world (as in James 1:27 or Mic. 6:8, above).

Contemptus Mundi

A monk is called to the way in which Christ's love prevails, the way of the cross. "Your way of acting should be different from the world's way; the love of Christ must come before all else" (*RB* 4). This theme of renunciation of the world weaves through the *Rule of St. Benedict* to the root of his story. As a young man, Benedict's rejection of the immorality in Rome prompts his retreat to solitary life. God calls all Christ-followers, whether cloistered away in monastic community or otherwise, to a different way of life—a life set apart or consecrated for his purposes. Again, this is not a hatred for the created world or its pleasures, good gifts from God which we should enjoy with gratitude. "For everything created by God is good, and nothing is to be rejected if it is received with gratitude" (1 Tim. 4:4).

Monastic rules are written for people who choose to live set apart from the world to varying degrees. But because each monastic community has some level of relation to the outside world, each includes instructions on how to conduct oneself in relation to the world. As mentioned above, Augustine presides over a small monastic community in the city of Hippo. Leaving their community on errand is a natural aspect of life. For these errands, Augustine advises, "There should be nothing about your clothing to attract attention. Besides, you should not seek to please by your apparel, but by a good life. . . . In your walk, deportment, and in all actions, let nothing occur to give offense to anyone who sees you, but only what becomes your holy state of life" (Pr. 4). For us the principle applies. As we live our lives, especially among those who don't know Christ, we ought to conduct ourselves in all holiness. Our conduct reflects on our Lord.

If Anyone Loves the World...

In contrast to the monks, we live in the world. We may live our days "in the world," but we are not "of" the world. We don't share the world's loves, so to speak. James characterizes embracing earthly ways of "making life work," such as greed, pride, or adultery, as friendship with the world and hostility toward God (James 4:4). The Apostle John writes in equally strong terms that if anyone loves the world, the love of the Father is not in him (1 John 2:15). "For all that is in the world, the lust of the flesh and the lust of the eyes and the boastful pride of life, is not from the Father, but is from the world" (1 John 2:16).

In the parable of the sower, Jesus warns that the worries of this world, the deceitfulness of riches, and desire for other things can both distract us and inhibit our fruitfulness (Mark 4:19). The Apostle Peter reminds us to separate from the loves of the world, "fleshly lusts which wage war against the soul" (1 Pet. 2:11). Likewise, 16th century reformer John Calvin cautions that worldly riches, power, and honors can so captivate us that we forget God. These things "dull people's keenness of sight by the glitter and seeming goodness they display . . . so that captivated by such tricks and drunk with such sweetness, they forget their God."[4] Tragically, like the Ephesian church in Revelation chapter 2, the things of this world can seduce us away from Christ, our first love.

One Love

God calls us to separate from the world because we have room for only one love. Centuries after Calvin, Dietrich Bonhoeffer asks us to consider whom we're really devoted to. Who or what is our first love? He cautions that worldly possessions can turn the hearts of the disciples away from Jesus. Unlike the Benedictine monks, worldly possessions are not forbidden to us, but the question remains: Where is our treasure? Does anything hinder us from loving God with all our heart? Bonhoeffer advises, "God and the world, God and its goods are incompatible, because the world and its goods make a bid for our hearts. . . . Our hearts have room only for one all-embracing devotion, and we can only cleave to one Lord. Every competitor to that devotion must be hated."[5]

We must choose. As much as we may try, we can't have one foot in the world and one foot in the kingdom of God. Our hearts have room for only one. Thomas à Kempis admonishes, "Keep yourself free from all worldly entanglement, and you will make good progress; but if you set great value on any worldly things, it will prove a great obstacle" (*IC* 2:5).

His words resemble the Apostle Paul's, who counts all things, even those considered gain by worldly measure, as loss for the sake of Christ. All is rubbish compared to knowing Christ (Phil. 3:8). With the enablement of God's Spirit, we make every effort to withdraw our hearts from the things of this world, to count them as nothing, and place our affections wholly on God. Thomas à Kempis exhorts us to "Strive to withdraw your heart from the love of visible things, and direct your affections to things invisible" (*IC* 1:1). In a similar vein, the Apostle Paul admonishes us to "keep seeking the things above, where Christ is. . . . Set your mind on the things above, not on the things that are on earth" (Col. 3:1–2).

Not only does a believer renounce the ways of this world, we cling to Christ. "No, *detachment* is not enough; we must go on to *attachment*. The detachment from the confusion all around us is in order to have a richer attachment to God."[6] We detach from the things of this world in order to attach more deeply to God. This single-mindedness pleases God and bears fruit in our life. "No soldier in active service entangles himself in the affairs of everyday life, so that he may please the one who enlisted him as a soldier" (2 Tim. 2:4).

Through the Cross We've Been Set Free

The world struggles under the power of the evil one (1 John 5:19). The reality? As followers of Christ, we too were formerly in bondage to the things of this world (Gal. 4:3). But through the cross the world has been "crucified" to us and we to the world (Gal. 6:14). Richard Foster describes the change in our daily lives when God breaks the power of the world over us.

> In the beginning God plucks the world out of our hearts—*contemptus mundi*. Here we experience a loosening of the chains of attachment to positions of prominence and power. All our longings for social recognition, to have our name in lights, begin to appear puny and trifling. We learn to let go of all control, all managing, all manipulation. We freely and joyfully live without guile. We experience a glorious detachment from this world and all it offers.[7]

Salvation in Christ brings great new freedom, a "spiritual severing of bonds." Those attachments and ambitions that once held such appeal—ambitions for prominence or power, inclinations to manipulate, control, or manage our lives, no longer hold sway. We see them for what they are—the world's feeble attempts at making life work. Through the cross God has broken the power of these things over us.

Spiritual formation, growth in holiness, is a lifelong process of *realizing* the new life at work within us. Daily we must walk in the reality of what God has accomplished in our hearts through the cross of Christ. Paul urges, "Do not be conformed to this world, but be transformed by the renewing of your mind" (Rom. 12:2). We're citizens and ambassadors of the kingdom of heaven (Phil. 3:20). Instead of conforming to the ways of this world, we need to allow the ways of God's kingdom to shape us. Each of us needs to discern how to live *in* the world, but not *of* the world (John 17:16). Every day Christ-followers actively live into the reality of who we are in him. God invites us to a life-giving way, "to deny ungodliness and worldly desires and to live sensibly, righteously and godly in the present age" (Titus 2:12). Above all, we depend on Christ for the ability to walk in a way that reflects the truth of who we are in him. God sent his only son Christ into the world "that we might live through Him" (1 John 4:9).

Amor Mundi

God calls his followers not only to reject the world's ways of doing things, but join with God in a deep love for the world. "Just when we have become free from it all, God hurls the world back into our heart—*amor mundi*—where we and God together carry the world in infinitely tender love. We deepen in our compassion for the bruised, the broken, the dispossessed. We ache and pray and labor for others in a new way, a selfless way, a joy-filled way."[8] What a beautiful picture as "we and God together carry the world in infinitely tender love," aching, praying, and laboring. This echoes the birthing imagery in Paul's deep caring for the Galatian people, "My children, with whom I am again in labor until Christ is formed in you" (Gal. 4:10). To love the world is to look on the world with the eyes of Christ, to love and serve and labor in prayer for those caught up in the world.

What is *amor mundi* in monastic context? Benedict's *Rule* specifically mentions the ministries of hospitality, prayer, and intercession. "All guests who present themselves are to be welcomed as Christ, for he himself will say: I was a stranger and you welcomed me" (*RB* 53). The abbot and brothers receive any guests with "the courtesy of love." They extend great care to their guests, particularly the poor and pilgrims, "Because in them more particularly Christ is received" (*RB* 53).

As one among many weary pilgrims, I myself experienced Benedictine hospitality when arriving late one afternoon at a monastery in a remote region of New Mexico. As instructed, I was aiming for a lunchtime arrival. But by the time I navigated the eighteen-mile, red-dirt road to its end, taking care not to venture off into the green river snaking alongside it, it was well past lunchtime. The compound was deathly quiet. I picked up my room key at the guesthouse and tried to slip into my room unnoticed. As I carried in my things, a young monk clad in a long brown robe warmly greeted me, asked me numerous times if I was hungry (I couldn't say no), and insisted upon taking me to the lunch hall. I sat alone in a grand room, admiring the great red stone bluffs outside and the colorful murals adorning the walls inside. Silently, the young brother and several of his colleagues proceeded to serve me a late lunch, extending every kindness.

Prior to Benedict, Basil of Caesarea oversaw small monastic communities in the region of Cappadocia (modern day Turkey). In about AD 370, he compiled a record of his advisory conversations with these communities called the *Great Asketikon*. His writings became the inspiration and foundation for Eastern monasticism. Basil emphasized the theme of love in his writings—loving God and loving others. Basil believed that community with other Christ-followers offers the best context for demonstrating love. And as an extension of our love for Christ, we serve the poor and needy. As bishop he developed the community of Basiliad, an extensive hospital and shelter staffed by devout men and women who cared for the sick, needy, and impoverished.

Over the centuries, monastic communities have served the world by offering hospitality, interceding for the world in their many hours of prayer, sending missionaries into the world, establishing schools, teaching, and caring for the neediest among us. The *Rule of the Society of Saint John the Evangelist* outlines the many ways in which a contemporary Anglican religious order serves the world. They minister through hospitality; offering retreats, workshops, and spiritual direction; preaching, teaching, and writing (including running a publishing company). They minister to persons with HIV/AIDS and to the poor. In their rule they articulate the following:

> God may call us to further the work of healing and reconciliation by reaching out to the sick, offering the sacraments of healing and forgiveness, befriending the alienated and perplexed, serving those in prison, and seeking the company of the marginalized. We are to be prepared for God to call us to be active witnesses for peace and social justice, bearing witness to Christ's presence on the side of people who are deprived and oppressed. We expect our calling to continue to bring special resources to bear on the needs and claims of children and their families in places where they are impoverished and at risk. [9]

As Christ so graciously and generously addresses the needs of others, so must we. We offer hospitality to strangers (Heb. 13:2). We share the hope of the gospel. Just as we have received, we extend Christ's mercy and compassion. We care for the poor, the sick, and the needy. We visit widows and orphans in their distress and those in prison. As we have means, we provide food, clothing, and shelter. And as we do these things, we do them unto Christ. "For I was hungry, and you gave Me something to eat; I was thirsty, and you gave Me something to drink; I was a stranger, and you invited Me in; naked, and you clothed Me; I was sick, and you visited Me; I was in prison, and you came to Me. . . . Truly I say to you, to the extent that you did it to one of these brothers of Mine, even the least of them, you did it to Me" (Matt. 25:35–40).

Contemptus Mundi and Amor Mundi in a World Adrift

These days the world, as evidenced in the predominant culture, seems untethered, drifting further and further from God. A recent survey, conducted by the Barna group confirms a deteriorating morality in the United States. In 2003 Barna measured attitudes of adults in America toward ten behaviors. Almost half of those surveyed indicated that a sexual relationship with someone other than their spouse was morally acceptable (42 percent). About one-third of survey respondents considered pornography (38 percent), profanity (36 percent), and drunkenness (35 percent) acceptable.[10] Barna makes some sobering conclusions. "The data trends indicate that the moral perspectives of Americans are likely to continue to deteriorate. . . . Compared to surveys we conducted just two years ago, significantly more adults are depicting such behaviors as morally acceptable."[11]

Concern also exists among those who self-identified as Christians. "Even most people associated with the Christian faith do not seem to have embraced biblical moral standards. Things are likely to get worse before they get better—and they are not likely to get better unless strong and appealing moral leadership emerges to challenge and redirect people's thoughts and behavior. At the moment, such leadership is absent."[12] This research reveals the very real struggle of self-professed Christ-followers to follow Christ's way of living *in* the world but not *of* the world.

As we have said, God calls us out of the world as a holy or set-apart people. We've been reconciled to God for the purpose of holiness. "He has now reconciled you . . . in order to present you before Him holy and blameless and beyond reproach" (Col. 1:22). The Greek word translated holy, *hagios*, essentially means separated—separated from sin and consecrated to God.[13] God admonishes us to walk blameless and innocent, children of God above reproach in a "crooked and perverse generation" (Phil. 2:15).

Not only does God call us to holiness in the world, but also to love (*amor mundi*). According to a study conducted by B.B. Warfield, in the

Bible the word "compassion" is used to describe Jesus' emotional disposition more frequently than any other.[14] We see one such example in the Gospel of Matthew. Jesus has been traveling through the villages, teaching in the synagogues, proclaiming the gospel of the kingdom, and healing their sicknesses. "Seeing the people, He felt compassion for them, because they were distressed and dispirited like sheep without a shepherd" (Matt. 9:36–38). Jesus' travels from village to village deeply move him. He's struck by the plight of his people. Again and again he finds them like sheep without a shepherd, neglected and betrayed by corrupt and heartless religious leaders. It seems that new leaders are needed. George Barna and others would argue that, based on their assessment, we need new leaders today. We need leaders who follow closely after Christ, living holy and virtuous lives, compelled by both compassion and charity.

A More Life-Giving Way

Our task this week is twofold. First, we want to examine our own hearts in relation to this dual relationship with the world. First, are there any ways you have become entangled in the world's ways? In what way do you need to separate from these things? Or, what does *contemptus mundi* look like in your life? Second, as you did in the previous chapter, consider the gifts, abilities, and resources which God has given you. What are some specific, even unique ways you can offer your time, talent, or treasure in the name of Christ? How do you feel led to extend Christ's love and compassion in the world (*amor mundi*)? For the spiritual discipline this week you'll have opportunity to actively serve those in need. We encourage you to serve with a friend, family members, or your Thrive Group.

Questions for Reflection and Discussion

1. **Reflect on the Word**

   Review the Sermon on the Mount (Matt. 5–7). Here Christ promotes an ethic, a way of life which runs counter to the world's way of doing things. List several examples of his "counter-cultural" proposal.

2. **Reflect on our world**

   How do you think the church is doing in terms of renouncing the world and living differently from the world? Where have we walked this well? Where have we struggled to live set apart from the world?

3. **Reflect on your spiritual journey**

   As a Christian, how have you struggled to live separately or differently from the world? In what ways have you found support for holy living?

4. **Reflect on your rule of life**

   In what ways have you become entangled in the world—caught up in worldly ambitions or attachments? How do you need to separate from these things? Or, what will *contemptus mundi* look like in your rule of life?

What are some specific ways you could offer your gifts, abilities, resources, or experiences to those in the world in the name of Christ? Or, what will *amor mundi* look like in your rule of life?

5. Complete Spiritual Discipline 9: Service.

Spiritual Discipline 9
Service

Whatever you do, do your work heartily, as for the
Lord rather than for men, knowing that from the Lord
you will receive the reward of the inheritance. It is the
Lord Christ whom you serve.

COLOSSIANS 3:23–24

Service is the "Loving, thoughtful, active promotion
of the good of others and the causes of God in our
world, through which we experience the many little
deaths of going beyond ourselves."

RICHARD FOSTER

Our Lord set the example. "The Son of Man did not come to be served,
but to serve, and to give His life a ransom for many" (Matt. 20:28). The
act of self-giving is at the heart of Christ's coming—serving God, mankind
and all of creation in the most selfless act of sacrificial service the world
has ever known.

Christ sets an example for us not only in death, but in life. At the
Last Supper, Jesus takes on the role of a servant. He pours water into a
basin, kneels down and washes the disciples' feet (John 13:3–5). An intimate act of humble service that takes our breath away. Just a few verses
earlier, John writes, "Having loved His own who were in the world, He
loved them to the end" (13:1). Christ loved us until the end of his earthly
life, and Christ loves us now as our risen Lord. Not only his words but
his deeds reveal this.

God invites us to serve in this remarkable way. In the Spirit of Christ we can extend his love to others, whether providing a warm meal or a new pair of shoes, or offering an embrace, a kind word or the hope of the gospel. Jesus said, "If I then, the Lord and the Teacher, washed your feet, you also ought to wash one another's feet. For I gave you an example that you also should do as I did to you" (John 13:14–15). Just as Christ, we ought to love and serve one another.

Just as Christ we go into the world. As God the Father sent Christ into the world, so Christ sends us (John 17:18).

> Now you, my brothers and sisters, are the eyes through which Christ's compassion is to look out upon this world, and yours are the lips through which His love is to speak; yours are the hands with which He is to bless men, and yours the feet with which He is to go about doing good—through His Church, which is His body.[15]

We prayerfully follow the example and leading of our Lord, humbly offering ourselves in loving service. How is Christ inviting you to serve others today?

As we have said, following Christ costs us something, but never as much as it cost our Lord. And the fruit of our good works, the good that is done, far outweighs the cost. Christ continues, "If you know these things, you are blessed if you do them" (John 13:17). Serving others is the way of true life.

But in the history of the church, practices such as service can also be undertaken as a spiritual discipline, an offering to God not only out of desire to serve him, but also to become more like Christ. "I will often be able to serve another simply as an act of love and righteousness, without regard to how it may enhance my abilities to follow Christ. . . . But I may also serve another to train myself away from arrogance, possessiveness, envy, resentment, or covetousness. In that case, my service is undertaken as a discipline for the spiritual life."[16] Out of love we serve God and others, but we can also serve as spiritual training or *askesis*, out of desire to "train away" vices such as envy or greed. We may serve out of a desire to grow in Christlike virtues such as compassion, joy, or gratitude.

Practicing service: In this chapter we discussed the corresponding themes of *contemptus mundi* and *amor mundi.* On the one hand, we've been called out of the world and its ways of making life work to live a different life, in service to God and his kingdom. We're not to love the world or the things of the world (1 John 2:15–16). Rather, as citizens of heaven we live as ambassadors of Jesus Christ to the world, offering his grace and truth.

This week take the opportunity to "go into the world" and serve in the name of Jesus, either individually, as a family, or as a Thrive Group. You might help serve a meal at a local homeless shelter, teach a Bible lesson, lead worship at a nursing home, or sort through donations at an area thrift store. Or perhaps someone in your group knows of a specific need of a neighbor or co-worker. Perhaps you could reach out to someone in your neighborhood in the name of Christ. It may be as simple as helping with yard work, buying some groceries, or inviting them to dinner. Be prepared to debrief your experience with your Thrive Group. How did God use your efforts? How did serving in such a way impact you? How did it stretch or challenge you?

Notes

[1.] N.T. Wright, *The Early Christian Letters For Everyone* (Louisville, Westminster John Knox Press, 2011), 147.

[2.] Thomas R. Kelly, *A Testament of Devotion* (New York, Harper and Brothers, 1941), 19.

[3.] Ibid.

[4.] John Calvin, *John Calvin: Selections from His Writings*, Harper Collins Spiritual Classics, (San Francisco: HarperOne, 2006), 103.

[5.] Bonhoeffer, *Cost of Discipleship*, 176.

[6.] Foster, *Celebration,* 21.

[7.] Richard Foster, *Spiritual Formation Agenda* http://www.christianitytoday.com/ct/2009/january/26.29.html.

8. Barna Research, "*Morality Conitunes to Decay*," Ibid.

9. *The Rule of the Society of Saint John the Evangelist* (Lanham, Md: Rowman and Littlefield, Inc., 1997), 3.

10. http://www.christianpost.com/news/morality-continues-to-decay-19837/.

11. Ibid.

12. Ibid.

13. Vines, 307.

14. B.B. Warfield, "The Emotional Life of Our Lord," available at http://www.monergism.com/thethreshold/articles/onsite/emotionallife.html.

15. Mark G. Pearse, as quoted in *Evangelical Christendom*, (London: Thomas George Johnson, 1888), 46.

16. Willard, *Spirit of the Disciplines*, 182.

CHAPTER 10

Discovering a More Life-Giving Way

The thief comes only to steal and kill and destroy;
I came that they might have life, and have it
abundantly.

JOHN 10:10

In his own words, Christ came to bring us life. A way of life enabled
by his abiding presence, full of his joy, ignited by faith, and marked
by self-giving. Christ cherishes us and invites us to a life in which we
truly thrive—a life lived with him. Yet in the day to day many of us experience anything but that kind of life. In contemporary culture the pace,
complexity, and pressures of life seem to escalate with each passing year.
We're harried and hurried and hungry for something more. Christ sees our
soul-weariness and invites us to a different way of life.

To discover a more life-giving way for today, you've traveled some
well-worn paths, with wisdom from Basil to Benedict to Bonhoeffer lighting the way. You've looked at your life, your values and priorities, gifts
and abilities, dreams and longings, your relationship with Christ and one
another, in light of an ancient way of life described in the little *Rule of St.
Benedict*. The Benedictine way finds its roots in the understanding that
true flourishing comes in abiding relationship with Jesus. The Benedictine
way finds its roots in love for Christ and a corresponding desire to draw
near to him, to become like him. In journeying along this ancient way,
I've invited you to discover rhythms, practices, and relationships which

draw you near to Christ. In the context of our chaotic 21st century times, not unlike Benedict's time, I've invited you to discover a way you can rise above the fray and truly thrive.

Along the way, we explored aspects of monastic life that draw us near to Christ: the virtue of fidelity, the discipline of attentiveness, prayer as priority, worship as a way of life, a rhythm of contemplation and action, dying to self and living for Christ, a community known by live, *contemptus mundi* and *amor mundi*. We considered the implications of these time-tested ideals for our life of faith today. We practiced spiritual disciplines which foster relationship with Jesus, practices such as scripture meditation, silence and solitude, *examen*, fixed-hour prayer, worship, rest, fasting, spiritual friendship, and service. In this last chapter, I invite you to bring together these experiences to write a simple rule of life—a gentle framework of rhythms, practices, and relationships which helps you draw near to Christ on a daily basis.

Over the next few months, as you engage in some devotional habits with some consistency, I pray our Lord will use these practices to help you increasingly notice and respond to his abiding presence in your life. As you grow closer to Christ, I pray you'll reflect his likeness more and more. I pray your love for God and others will deepen. If you've worked through this material with a Thrive Group or spiritual friend, I encourage you to stay in touch. God has hardwired us for community. Discuss how you can continue to support one another in your mutual desire to follow Christ and grow in likeness to him.

As many of us know all too well, without intentionality we can find our lives ordered around any number of things. A rule of life offers a gentle guideline for ordering life around relationship with Jesus. This is the remarkable, life-changing way to which Christ invites us, the "with-God" life. As we have noted, a rule of life is not about keeping rules, but keeping this relationship.

As you come to the end of this material and pen your own rule of life, I pray you pursue with intentionality the God who loves you, who calls you beloved. May you discern and live deeply into those rhythms, practices, and relationships that nurture the relationship in which we truly flourish and find life. May it be your lifelong endeavor to live more deeply each day into this extraordinary relationship, and may the Lord Jesus Christ lead and bless you in such a noble effort. Like a tree planted by flowing streams, bringing forth its fruit in season, I pray you thrive in your own unique and beautiful way, as God has always intended.

Spiritual Discipline 10
Discerning a Rule of Life

You will make known to me the path of life;
In Your presence is fullness of joy.

PSALM 16:11

For the final spiritual discipline, you'll write a simple rule of life for the near term—the next season, semester, or few months. This exercise provides an opportunity to synthesize the work you've done in each chapter and write a rule that reflects the kind of life you believe Christ invites you to live. This final exercise provides an opportunity to identify a loose framework of rhythms, practices, and relationships that helps you draw near to Christ on a daily basis.

This week you'll want to prayerfully review your work in each chapter. If you met with a Thrive Group or spiritual friend to discuss this material, you'll gather one last time to share your rule of life with each other, offer prayer and encouragement, and discuss how you can support one another in abiding by your rule of life.

Philosophy and Practice

Your rule should contain two parts. First, you'll want to write down your big picture ideals or scriptural basis for how you want to follow Christ in the day to day. What's important to you? You may choose to incorporate a central metaphor to communicate this to others, but you'll want to include such things as several personally significant scriptures, core beliefs, values, longings, priorities, and why these particular ideals or guiding principles undergird your rule. These are big questions. Be prayerful and thoughtful and ask the Spirit of God to reveal these things to you. If this is your first time to write a rule, you may just discover bits and pieces now, but know that abiding by a rule of life is a lifelong practice, a discipline you can grow into year after year.

Second, you'll identify a few rhythms, practices, and devotional habits that you would like to establish with some regularity to nurture your relationship with God. For the purpose of this exercise, *you need only define this in the short term.* In other words, what will the next season, semester, or few months look like?

It's appropriate to periodically evaluate and revise your rule so plan on doing so three or four months from now. You'll probably find it helpful to revisit your rule several times a year, particularly as aspects of your life change, whether relationally, vocationally, or otherwise. You may choose to revise some aspects of your rule while other aspects of your rule may carry over unchanged.

For now, identify a few daily, weekly, or monthly disciplines you desire to practice with consistency *over the next few months.* In the short term you might identify particular scriptures or devotional materials you want to emphasize in your personal study or meditation, and several prayer practices to incorporate. You might identify an area of desired growth, some relational priorities, and ways of serving or offering your gifts. You might begin by writing down any life-giving rhythms, practices, and relationships that are already a part of your life.

For convenience, the Rule of Life questions from previous chapters are reprinted in Appendix A (following). Also see Appendix B for a simple rule of life template to help you order your rule. Finally, see appendices C, D, and E for example rules of life, written by Christ-followers who've worked through this guidebook just like you.

A few general guidelines: Keep it simple. A rule of life is not meant to be complicated or burdensome. A rule of life simply offers the opportunity for more intentionality in our relationship with Jesus. Second, be realistic. Consider which rhythms and practices would be reasonable for your particular season of life and personality type. A small step in the right direction is still a step. Just do what you can.

Third, remember the corporate nature of ancient monastic rules. Which communities are you a part of? How will the rhythms, practices, and relationships in your local church shape your rule? It may be new to you, but consider following the rhythm of the church calendar, which follows the life, death, and resurrection of Christ. How will the rhythms, practices, and relationships of your family shape your rule? Perhaps this is the opportunity to establish some life-giving rhythms and practices for your family.

In presenting your rule to your group, let your creativity shine. Present your rule in whatever form you find helpful, a form that best communicates your desires and intentions. Finally, as with the Christian life, remember the journey itself offers great value. You may not feel completely happy with the rule you pen, but embrace what you've learned along the way. Celebrate the progress you've made so far. Discovering a more life-giving way is in many respects a lifelong process. I pray your experience of life in Christ will deepen each day, becoming your lifelong joy.

APPENDIX A:

Questions to Consider When Writing a Rule of Life

1: Benedict of Nursia: An Unlikely Guide for the Journey

a. Which scriptures will form the philosophy or foundation of my rule? Why?

b. Over the next three or four months, how do I want to regularly engage with the Bible? Which particular scriptures will I emphasize? Which particular devotional, resources, or tools might be helpful?

2: Fidelity to Christ

a. What are my core values or guiding principles (five or six)? How might these values relate to my life story?

b. How do I want my rule of life to reflect my values (what's important to me)?

c. In what area of life is God inviting me to fidelity? What are some tangible ways I can live in faithfulness to Christ?

3: Attending to Our Relationship with the Lord

a. Which spiritual disciplines will I practice to develop greater attentiveness to God's presence and activity in my life (God-awareness)?

b. Which spiritual disciplines will I practice to develop greater attentiveness to my own soul (self-awareness)?

4: Prayer as Priority

    a. Which personal priorities will order my rule of life in the near term?

    b. How will my daily life (or rule of life) reflect my priorities?

    c. How will prayer have priority in my way of life? Which prayer practices do I want to include in my rule?

5: Worship as a Way of Life

    a. What place will worship play in my rule of life? What are some ways I can cultivate a heart of worship?

6: A Rhythm of Contemplation and Action

    a. Breathing in: In my rule of life, how will I incorporate contemplation, or soul-restoring practices?

    b. Breathing out: In my rule of life, how will I incorporate action, or giving out of what I receive from Christ?

7: Dying to Self and Living for Christ

    a. What is one way I believe God is calling me to die to self and live for Christ? Or, what is one way I desire to grow in virtue or likeness to Christ?

    b. What are some specific practices or disciplines which could support this?

    c. What kind of accountability or support would help? Who could provide accountability or support?

8: A Community Known by Love

    a. Who are the significant people in my life right now (family members, spiritual friends, colleagues, those with whom you worship or serve)?

    b. Over the next three or four months, how can I better attend to these relationships?

c. In the church where I worship and serve, what are our corporate or shared rhythms and practices? How do these rhythms and practices relate to my rule of life?

d. Which spiritual disciplines or regular rhythms would I like to practice with my family?

e. How can I steward my God-given gifts, abilities, experiences, and resources in the church?

9: Contemptus Mundi and Amor Mundi

a. Are there ways I've become entangled in the world—caught up in the world's ways of "making life work"? How do I need to separate from these things? Or, what will *contemptus mundi* look like in my rule of life?

b. What are some specific ways I can offer my gifts, abilities, resources, and experience in the name of Christ? Or, what will *amor mundi* look like in my rule of life?

APPENDIX B

Worksheet:
A Rule of Life for the Next Few Months

Below is a guide for writing a rule of life for the next season, semester, or few months. This template orders around three basic aspects of life: rhythms, practices, and relationships.

Before writing your rule, take time to prayerfully discern what kind of life Christ invites you to live in this season. Which aspects of life will continue? Where is Christ inviting change or growth? How will your core values, personality, and personal priorities shape your rule?

A. Rhythms. Consider the larger rhythms of your life. What will a rhythm of contemplation and action look like (breathing in and breathing out)? How could your life reflect a more life-giving and God-honoring rhythm?

Daily.

Weekly.

This semester or season.

B. Practices. Which practices help you draw near to Christ? Or, what's life-giving or soul-nourishing for you? Make some notes here, then narrow down your list. Which practices are for this season?

Scripture. How will you engage with God's Word for the next few months? Identify a specific Bible book, online guide, devotional book and/or study partner(s).

Prayer. How will you pray? Consider the ACTS model: Adoration, Confession, Thanksgiving, and Supplication. Or, consider praying scripture, fixed-hour prayers, a breath prayer (a one-line prayer prayed throughout the day), or finding a prayer partner.

Service. Who will you serve in this season? How will you serve? Questions to help you discern an area of service or gifting.
1. What are you most passionate about contributing to the body of Christ?
2. What do you consider the most pressing need in the church or world today?
3. Where have you seen your efforts bear fruit?
4. What gifts and abilities have others affirmed in you?

C. **Relationships.** Who can you partner with for mutual encouragement and support in this season? Where and when will you meet?

Spiritual Friendship. Four questions spiritual friends might ask:
1. How is it with your soul?
2. Where are you noticing God's presence lately?
3. How is God inviting you to respond to what you are noticing?
4. How can I pray for you?

APPENDIX C:

Sample Rule of Life 1

My life-guiding scripture: "And you shall love the Lord your God with all your heart, and with all your soul, and with all your mind, and with all your strength. . . . You shall love your neighbor as yourself."

MATTHEW 12:30–31

1. Fidelity to Christ:
Read D.A. Carson's *For the Love of God* and reflect on the scriptures daily.

2. Attending to My Relationship with the Lord:
Practice the spiritual disciplines of *examen* and solitude and silence to deepen fellowship with the Lord and awareness of his presence.

3. Prayer as Priority:
Besides ongoing prayer throughout the day, intercede for others during my daily commute and when the Holy Spirit brings them to mind. Read and pray through *Valley of Vision* (a compilation of Puritan prayers) on the weekend to enjoy the beauty and heritage of historic prayers. Pray with my husband in the evenings.

4. Worship as a Way of Life:
Enjoy literature, museums, art, and walks in creation. Listen to praise music on my iPod. Attend weekly worship services.

5. **A Rhythm of Contemplation and Action:**
Contemplation: Practice the discipline of rest. Take nature walks and "beauty breaks" (taking time to enjoy beauty in museums, music, nature, art, or literature).[1]

Action: Serve my husband and children through practicing presence and serving as the Lord leads. Serve as a writer at church. Continue graduate studies, mentoring, and fostering spiritual formation among ministry leaders.

6. **Dying to Self and Living for Christ:**
Practice fasting from sugar or technology. Record insights from the Lord in my fasting journal. Maintain accountability through spiritual friendships.

7. **A Community Known by Love:**
Attend church with my husband. Spend time with family, significant friends, and others through date nights, phone calls, coffee dates, and fellowship with other couples monthly.

8. **Contemptus Mundi and Amor Mundi:**
Abstain from online shopping. Fast, as I'm prompted by the Spirit. Simplify possessions by sorting through our closets this summer.

Notes:

[1] The term "beauty breaks" originates with my dear friend, Shelley Frew.

APPENDIX D:

Sample Rule of Life 2

My Core Values

- Work for my household – economic welfare
- Care for my family – support their journeys
- Health and fitness – intentional decisions and habits
- Learning continuously – mental and spiritual health
- Selflessness – with time, talent, and treasure

My Priorities

- Vertical alignment (with God)
- Horizontal work (service to others)
- Attentiveness
- Obedience

My Spiritual Discipline Focus

- *Examen*: practicing awareness of God's presence and of my own soul
- Solitude every day
- Prayer every day
- Scripture meditation every day

My Emphases Going Forward

- **Dying to Self and Living for Christ**
  - ❏ Practice self-denial and fasting regularly.
  - ❏ "Bring more of myself to my grace relationship with God."
- **Contemptus Mundi and Amor Mundi**
  - ❏ Practice "turning loose of earthly attachments and ambitions."
  - ❏ "Deepen my compassion and concern for the world."

APPENDIX E:

Sample Rule of Life 3

Walk with me and work with me—watch how I do it.
Learn the unforced rhythms of grace. I won't lay anything heavy or ill-fitting on you. Keep company with
me, and you'll learn to live freely and lightly.

MATTHEW 11:28, *THE MESSAGE*

Daily I desire to live my life in this way:

- Beginning in the morning, I will meet my Lord on my knees (Ps. 4:3).
- In the morning I will open his Word and meditate (Ps. 4:4–5, Matt. 6:11). For the next three months, I'll study the Psalms and the Gospel of John each day.
- I desire to walk with gratitude and praise each day, as an act of worship (Isa. 61:3, Lam. 3:22).
- By God's grace, I will open my eyes and pay attention to his gifts and presence all around me. Even in my mortal helplessness and blindness, I will search for his leading (Ps. 4:3, Isa. 42:16).
- By God's grace, I will set aside one to four hours on Tuesdays for silence and solitude (Ps. 1:2, 145:5).
- By God's grace, I will fast once a month for fixed-hour prayer and as a means to grow in temperance (Ps. 91:1, Gal. 5:22–23).

- I will meet my Lord daily in prayer for one or more of the following: praise, thanksgiving, intercession, supplication, and peace in his presence (Ps. 17:1, 46:10).
- I will meet with friends in town or e-mail out-of-town friends for life-giving joy and fellowship!
- I will serve God through serving others. I will attend to my family's needs, including my husband, our children, their spouses, my precious grandchildren, my brother, as well as women's ministry at our church, and my dear friend in California. When I offer grace or mercy or some form of care to another person, it is life-giving for me!

APPENDIX F

Thrive Group Leader Guide

This material lends itself well to a small group format in an eleven-week time frame (eleven weekly meetings). Allow about two hours for each group session. For the first week, bring everyone together for a casual dinner and fellowship. Ask each person to share what brings them to the group and one way you all can pray for them over the next eleven weeks. At the first meeting you'll find it beneficial to write a simple Thrive Group Rule. As a group, take time to identify five or six shared values, ideals, or practices you want to uphold as a community. For example, the group might agree to maintain confidentiality, share authentically, listen well, and pray regularly for each other. Create a brief document outlining your corporate ideals, sign it, and make a copy for each group member. As part of your rule, you might choose a group leader or agree to take turns leading the group conversation each week. Close the session in prayer. Note that for the second meeting you'll read Chapter 1, complete the chapter questions, read the Introduction to Spiritual Disciplines, and practice Spiritual Discipline 1.

In the second through tenth meetings, you'll meet for prayer and discussion about each chapter, corresponding questions, and spiritual discipline. In the second week's discussion (of Chapter 1), you'll want to allow time for identifying the rhythms, practices, and relationships that make up each person's current "rule" or way of life. Invite each person to share observations of their current way of life, both what they find life-giving and what they might like to change in some way.

The final meeting offers a time of celebration, ideally around a meal. After dinner, invite each person to share highlights of their rule of life. Depending on the size of the group, you may decide to take two weeks for this exercise. You might find it beneficial to each bring a "spiritual artifact" to share with the group, an object symbolizing your spiritual journey over the past eleven weeks. After the meal, allow each person the opportunity to share their spiritual artifact and highlights of their rule of life for the purpose of prayer, encouragement, and support. After each person shares, ask how the group can support and pray for them in abiding by their rule of life. Finally, discuss how the group might continue to encourage one another, whether through sharing their progress and prayer requests through e-mails or texts, or meeting once a month for dinner.

A Typical Group Session

Opening Each Session

I suggest you begin each Thrive Group session with a brief spiritual practice. This aids everyone in setting aside the activities of their day and entering into the group conversation with more presence. Perhaps you could start by lighting a candle and practicing several minutes of silence. Or perhaps you, or someone in your group, could offer a brief prayer inviting God's presence or the group's attentiveness to God and to each other. Your weekly prayer might simply be, Come, Lord Jesus. Or perhaps you might pray together a familiar prayer such as the Collect for Purity from *The Book of Common Prayer* (see Spiritual Discipline 3) or lead the group through scripture meditation (or *lectio divina*, see Spiritual Discipline 1). After the practice of *lectio divina*, give each person the opportunity to share any significant insights that came to mind during the reading.

How Is It with Your Soul?

After the opening spiritual discipline, give each person the opportunity to talk about their spiritual journey since you last met. As noted in the Preface, there are three questions which you could ask at each meeting: How is it with your soul (how are you really)? Where have you been noticing God lately? And, how is God inviting you to respond to what you are noticing? Approach these conversations with sensitivity. Sometimes the answer to a question may be "I don't know." Regularly reflecting on these questions can help us develop spiritual attentiveness—both to God's presence in our life and to how we respond to his presence. Chapter 3 discusses the importance of attentiveness in the spiritual life.

Discussing the Weekly Session and Spiritual Discipline

Next it's appropriate to discuss the chapter reading, questions, and your experience of practicing the spiritual discipline. You might open by reading something from the chapter and ask the group to respond. Ask the group to share aspects of the reading that spoke to them. Where were they encouraged? Where were they challenged? Where did it seem that life and the reading intersected this week? After discussing the chapter reading, move on to the Questions for Reflection and Discussion, particularly the ones related to your rule of life.

Finally, share your experience of the weekly spiritual discipline. What was it like to practice this particular discipline? Was this discipline beneficial or life-giving for you? Why or why not? In what ways was it helpful? In what ways was it difficult or challenging? What did you learn about yourself in the process?

As with any small group, the conversation will ebb and flow. Natural pauses or times of silence provide opportunities to reflect, process, and listen to the Spirit of God. Resist the urge to jump into these times. On the other hand, at times you may sense the need to stop the conversation and pause for a short silence. In that case, you might say something like, "Let's take this into silence" or "Let's take a few minutes to pray silently."

One additional note, I've included a number of questions throughout the chapter readings. You might encourage your group to highlight or underline the questions as they read. As you all feel led, it might be beneficial to incorporate some of these questions into your weekly conversation.

Closing Prayer

Close the meeting with prayer. Take time for each group member to share a specific way the group can pray for them this week, particularly in relation to being more intentional and attentive in our spiritual lives. Be sensitive to your group. If group members are just learning to pray out loud with others, you might offer the closing prayer. Or, simply ask them to write a one-sentence prayer request on a note card and pass the card to another group member. Then go around the circle and ask each member to pray for the request (just reading it is fine). Over time, as everyone grows more comfortable, you can adjust the way you pray. After sharing personal prayer requests, close with a familiar prayer like the Lord's Prayer.

GLOSSARY OF TERMS

Amor mundi
A Latin phrase meaning "love for the world," joining with God in a deep compassion and concern for persons who are caught up in an orientation toward life which is hostile toward God.

Contemplation
Focused and sustained attention, a heightened awareness and openness to God, often including a sense of awe and wonder.

Contemptus mundi
A Latin phrase meaning "contempt for the world," detachment from or renunciation of a way of life that draws us away from God.

Core values
Those particular ideals, notions, or guiding principles that hold great importance for you. Often these ideals emerge from our life experiences or stories.

Examen of conscience
The spiritual discipline of noticing how I respond to God's presence and activity in my daily life.

Examen of consciousness
The spiritual discipline of noticing God's presence and activity in my daily life.

Fasting
A spiritual discipline in which we abstain from the fulfillment of a normal or legitimate desire for the purpose of drawing near to God. Fasting provides opportunity for God to place certain desires in proper perspective in our lives.

Fixed-hour prayer	An ordering rhythm one prays at set times during the day as a means of turning our attention and affection toward God.
Life-giving	Anything that draws us near to Christ. Here we're particularly focused on rhythms, practices, and relationships that draw us near to Christ.
Rule of life	A gentle guideline that helps us order the rhythms, practices, and relationships of our lives around our relationship with Jesus, to live in a way that is life-giving and God-honoring. A rule of life is not about rule keeping; it's about relationship keeping, attending closely to a life-giving relationship with Jesus Christ.
Scripture meditation	Reading the scriptures slowly, prayerfully, and attentively with the expectation of a personal insight from God.
Silence and solitude	The spiritual practice of withdrawing from the company of others to be alone with God in silence and quietness of soul.
Sola gratia	A Latin phrase meaning "grace alone" associated with Reformers like Martin Luther, which emphasizes that the whole of the spiritual life is empowered and enabled by God's grace.
Soul	An immaterial aspect of a human being which integrates the various components of a person, the essence of a person; sometimes used in reference to the person as a whole.
Spiritual Discipline	A means of drawing near to Jesus and attending to our relationship with him. These practices

provide opportunity for God to regularly nourish, strengthen, and restore our souls through our engaging with him in a way that is personal and intentional.

Spiritual friendship   A relationship between Christ-followers in which the objective is to accompany, support, and pray for one another in attending and responding to God's presence and activity in their life.

Spiritual formation   The process by which God progressively forms Christ-followers in his likeness through a life-giving relationship with God, enabled by the presence and power of his gracious indwelling Spirit. We experience holistic transformation, a heart change that manifests in the way we live our lives.

AFTERWORD

The Way to Thrive

In the 20th century, sometimes the church forgot to tell the whole story. There was a lot of emphasis on "getting saved" (what some people jokingly referred to as "fire insurance") and "going to heaven," but not enough emphasis on how relationship with Christ changes our life today. God has made us to flourish and thrive. From now into eternity. That's the passion that drove the publication of this book. God invites us to experience a more life-giving way beginning now, not just in the world to come. Maybe you're curious to know more of my story and how Christ invited me to thrive. Well, pull out the French press and make yourself a real cup of coffee.

When I was a child, I was cautious and fearful. I think I carried so much fear because, although I grew up in a loving home, one of my siblings suffered from an undiagnosed mental illness. His internal chaos spilled over into all of our lives. My parents tried hard to help him, but they didn't begin to know how. None of us did.

When I was fifteen a friend invited me into a community of youth that followed Jesus Christ. The first thing that attracted me to them was their love. It was compelling. And real. I wanted to belong to this community of love and acceptance. Over time I learned that the love of these brothers and sisters was an outpouring of the love they knew in the person of Jesus Christ.

I too began to know Jesus' love and the story of his life, death, and resurrection as told in the scriptures from Genesis to Revelation, God's love letter to us. I began to understand that we all live within a grand and glorious story that an extraordinarily good and loving God is personally and actively writing—the story of creation, fall, incarnation, re-creation, and renewal. It's a story that God has written in the heart of every person.

Creation

God has always existed in a perfectly loving, mutually self-giving community of three Persons—Father, Son, and Spirit. Three Persons. One God. Yes, this is a great mystery. But the love that exists in this community is so profuse and profound that God wants to share it with others. In an outpouring of that love God created the world. In an outpouring of that love God created people. He lovingly shaped us in his likeness to receive and respond to his love. God created us for relationship with him, to enjoy and delight in him, to flourish and thrive, to love and be loved forever. He would be our God and we would be his people. God created each of us not only to experience his love each day, but to extend his love, peace, and justice to the world in compelling and creative and extravagant ways, just like he does.

But God doesn't want to force us to love him. Love that is forced is not love at all, but obligation. God invites each of us to a relationship with him, but we have a choice.

Fall

This part of the story is more familiar, but along the way every one of us, all the way back to Adam and Eve, has chosen to turn away from God. It's tragic but, each of us has stepped out from under God's benevolent rule. Thinking that we know better, we've chosen to go it alone, to chart our own course, to do things our way. Sadly, I realize that I too have been filled with that same awful pride, thinking that I know better than God. It's the terrible trajectory of human history, isn't it? We've rejected the very God who created us, forgetting that God is compassionate, kind, and good.

We forget that he's slow to anger, abounding in loving-kindness, working toward our well-being and flourishing.

Things haven't gone so well. All the way back to Adam and Eve, when we chose our own way we broke relationship with God. God is holy and sinless and there can be no fellowship between darkness and light. Or you could think of it this way, when we choose to do things our way, we cut ourselves off from God like branches broken off a vine, withering on the trellis. I know it sounds harsh, but when we choose a different way than what we're made for—God's way of love and self-giving, we begin to die. In fact, the scriptures tell us that the tragic fruit of our rebellion is death (Rom. 6:23).

To put it another way, we were made for relationship with God. God is the source of all life. When we choose to cut God out of the picture, we experience the fruit of that—selfishness, greed, jealousy, broken relationships, heartache, hatred, suffering, sickness, and war. The list is long and ugly and everywhere. To make matters worse, not only is this good and beautiful world being corrupted by our sin, but there's a destructive power, a contrarian power of sheer evil actively promoted by the devil, the chief rebel. He breathes lies and denies God and the goodness of God at every possible turn. He is powerful, wreaking havoc in the world, and all too often we play along. And contrary to God, who seeks our flourishing, the enemy seeks our destruction (John 10:10).

Incarnation

With all the anarchy and destruction in the world because of sin and evil, we were in desperate need. God knew this, and when our relationship with God was broken by the very first sin, God had already planned an intervention. He saw it coming. We see a hint of God's plan all the way back in the Garden of Eden. In their pride Adam and Eve disobeyed God. In the aftermath of that catastrophe God tells the devil, "I will put enmity between you and the woman, and between your seed and her seed; He shall bruise you on the head, and you shall bruise him on the heel" (Gen. 3:15). What did God mean? One day the devil would "bruise the heel" of the woman's seed, Jesus. One day he would cause harm to Jesus. However, one day Jesus, the coming King and Savior, would bruise the serpent on the head, fatally wounding him. One day Christ would put an end to the devil and his evil and destructive agenda.

Thousands of years later, when the time was right, God sent Jesus to earth to restore relationship between God and the people he created. Jesus was uniquely both fully God and fully human. In the most humble of ways he entered into the human condition, proclaiming the coming of God's kingdom, calling people to repent or turn from going their own way and return to God. Jesus brought foretastes or glimpses of the kingdom that God would one day establish in full. In the person of Jesus, God dwelled among us with great compassion, healing the sick, casting out demons, and offering forgiveness and freedom from sin.

Jesus lived a sinless life from first to last, a life characterized by perfect love. Out of love for the Father and love for us, Jesus died the death that each of us deserved because of our sin (Rom. 6:23). Remarkably, in his body Jesus suffered the consequences of the sins of the whole world. He did this so that we could be forgiven and reconciled with God. It really is more than we can fathom, but this is what Jesus did. In Jesus Christ we've been forgiven and reconciled to God. And our part is merely to trust in Jesus, to believe and receive the gift he freely gives. If you haven't already, you can show your trust in a simple prayer to God, asking for forgiveness and inviting Jesus into your life. At your invitation, Christ enters into your spirit, dwells within you, and from that point everything changes! We begin to truly flourish in a life-giving relationship with Jesus.

Re-creation

Jesus not only lived and died for us, he rose from the dead. There's so much more to this story. Not only are we forgiven and reconciled to God because of Jesus' death on our behalf, we're made new through his resurrection. This is exciting. God gradually remakes us in Christ's image. Remember, mankind was created in God's image. But over the years, sin distorted his image in us. Some might say we were barely recognizable as his children.

But when we trust in Christ by faith, we receive his Spirit, who lives in us and animates and influences our ways. God begins to change us from the inside out. As we talked about in this book, there are things we can do to foster relationship with Christ, but he enables it all. As we've seen, God's Spirit can work through our simple acts of loving attention to him—prayer, worship, scripture meditation, silence, solitude, or service. Over time, as we cooperate with God's Spirit, he gradually remakes us in image and likeness to Christ. Thankfully, God helps us to follow him every step of the way. His Spirit works in us to both desire and follow his ways (Phil. 2:13).

This is a lot to take in. What I discovered at age fifteen and what many discovered before me, is that real life, the true way of human flourishing, is found in Jesus Christ. Jesus is the way, the truth, and the life and the only way we can reconcile with God the Father (John 14:6). Entering into a relationship with God in Jesus is both life-changing and life-giving, the beginning of a glorious adventure that goes beyond this life into eternity.

Renewal

The story of God's remarkable love brings me tremendous hope. It's the hope that I held onto through the brokenness I experienced in my birth family. It's the hope I held onto through my own cancer and a loved one's long struggle with alcohol and every other challenge of life. It's the hope I hold onto now as I look around the world and see brokenness and pain and suffering every day. It can be overwhelming to see these things.

Things are not yet the way they are supposed to be, but God is at work. Embracing Jesus' act of selfless love can profoundly change life as we know and live it. With the help of his indwelling Spirit we can live as his image bearers, embodying love and justice and peace in this world. What

God asks of us can be summed up in two commands—love God and love your neighbor as yourself. This is our mission to the world with the help of God's Spirit. This is the story I want to help write. It's the very thing that attracted me to Jesus so many years ago—love.

But there is one final act in this story. All of creation has been distorted by the sin and evil in the world. We can still see beauty around us, but it pales in comparison to what it will be. One day Christ will return and complete the work he began so many years ago. One day he will completely restore all of creation. He'll make everything new. Christ will return triumphant and end the tyranny of sin, evil, and death forever. The kingdom of God and the reign of Christ, characterized by peace, justice, and love, will come to earth in all its fullness. This is the future that God is moving all of creation toward. This is the future God wants all of his people to choose and work toward. He writes about this renewed creation in the book of Revelation.

> Then I saw a new heaven and a new earth; for the first heaven and the first earth passed away, and there is no longer any sea. . . . And I heard a loud voice from the throne, saying, "Behold, the tabernacle of God is among men, and He will dwell among them, and they shall be His people, and God Himself will be among them, and He will wipe away every tear from their eyes; and there will no longer be any death; there will no longer be any mourning, or crying, or pain; the first things have passed away" (Rev. 21:1–4).

One day, God will remake all things and this renovated world will be the place of God's glory, where we'll live forever with God. God will dwell in perfect love with the people. God will finish his work in us and we will become fully human—everything God made us to be. There will be no more suffering or sickness or pain. He will be our God and we will be his people. Maranatha. Come, Lord Jesus.

BIBLIOGRAPHY

Allender, Dan B. *To Be Told: God Invites You to Coauthor Your Future*. Colorado Springs: Waterbrook Press, 2005.

Arndt, W.F. and F.W. Gingrich. *A Greek-English Lexicon of the New Testament and Other Early Christian Literature*. Chicago: University of Chicago, 1957.

Augustine of Hippo. *The Confessions,* Vintage Spiritual Classics. New York: Vintage, 1998.

Bakke, Jeannette A. *Holy Invitations*. Grand Rapids, MI: Baker Books, 2000.

Barton, Ruth Haley. *Sacred Rhythms: Arranging Our Lives for Spiritual Transformation*. Downers Grove, IL: InterVarsity Press, 2006.

Basil of Caesarea. *Letter 2 to Gregory of Nazianzus*, The St. Pachomius Orthodox Library, Sept-Oct 1995. Available at http://www.voskrese.info/spl/basil2.html 2.

Benedict of Nursia. *The Rule of Saint Benedict,* trans. Anthony C. Meisel and del Mastro. New York: Doubleday, 1975.

_____. *The Rule of Saint Benedict*. Vintage Spiritual Classics. New York: Vintage Books, 1998.

Benner, David G. *Sacred Companions*. Downers Grove, IL: IVP, 2002.

Bonner, Gerald. *Saint Augustine: The Monastic Rules,* The Augustine Series, Vol. IV. Hyde Park, N.Y.: New City Press, 2004.

Bonhoeffer, Dietrich. *Life Together.* San Francisco, CA: Harper San Francisco, 1976.

_____. *The Cost of Discipleship.* New York: Touchstone, 1995.

Bromiley, Geoffrey W. *Theological Dictionary of the New Testament.* Grand Rapids: William B. Eerdmans, 1985.

Calhoun, Adele Ahlberg. *Spiritual Disciplines Handbook: Practices that Transform Us.* Downers Grove, IL: InterVarsity Press, 2005.

Calvin, John. *John Calvin: Selections from His Writings,* Harper Collins Spiritual Classics. San Francisco: HarperOne, 2006.

Fenelon, Francois. *Spiritual Progress,* Christian Classics Ethereal Library. Available at http://www.ccel.org/ccel/fenelon/progress.v.xvi.html.

Foster, Richard J. *Celebration of Discipline: The Path to Spiritual Growth.* Third Edition. San Francisco: Harper San Francisco, 1988.

_____. *Prayer: Finding the Heart's True Home.* San Francisco: HarperCollins, 1992.

_____. "Spiritual Formation Agenda" Christianity Today (January 2009). Available at http://www.christianitytoday.com/ct/2009/january/26.29.html.

Greenman, Jeffrey. "Spiritual Formation in Theological Perspective," in *Life in the Spirit,* ed. J. Greenman and G. Kalantzis. Downers Grove: InterVarsity, 2010.

Gregory the Great. *The Book of Pastoral Rule,* trans. by George E. Demacopoulos. Crestwood, NJ: St.Vladimir's Seminary Press, 2007.

Hall, Christopher. "Reading Christ in the Heart," in *Life in the Spirit,* ed. J. Greenman and G. Kalantzis. Downers Grove: InterVarsity, 2007.

Hipps, Shane. *Flickering Pixels: How Technology Shapes Your Faith.* Grand Rapids: Zondervan, 2009.

Kardong, Terrence, *The Benedictines.* Wilmington: Michael Glazer, Inc., 1988.

_____. "Work Is Prayer: Not!" *Assumption Abbey Newsletter,* October 1995. Available from http://www.osb.org/gen/topics/work/kard1.html.

Kelly, Thomas R. *A Testament of Devotion.* New York: Harper Brothers, 1941.

Kenneson, Philippiansip. *Life on the Vine: Cultivating the Fruit of the Spirit in Christian Community.* Downers Grove: IVP, 1999.

Ladrigan-Whelpley, Theresa. "Benedict of Nursia: Rule," in *Christian Spirituality: The Classics,* ed. Arthur G. Holder. London: Routledge, 2009.

McKnight, Scot. Fasting. Nashville: Thomas Nelson, 2009.

_____. *Praying with the Church.* Brewster, MA: Paraclete Press, 2006.

Nouwen, Henri. *The Way of the Heart.* New York: HarperCollins, 1991.

Owen, John. *The Works of John Owen,* ed. William H. Goold, 24 vols. (1850–1855; Edinburgh: Banner of Truth Trust, 1965–1991), 3:405, as quoted in K. Kapic, "Evangelical Holiness," in *Life in the Spirit,* ed. J. Greenman and G. Kalantzis. Downers Grove: InterVarsity, 2007.

Peterson, Eugene. *Eat This Book: A Conversation in the Art of Spiritual Reading.* Grand Rapids: Eerdmans, 2006.

_____. *The Contemplative Pastor.* Grand Rapids, MI: William B. Eerdmans, 1989.

Sittser, Gerald. *Water from a Deep Well.* Downers Grove: InterVarsity, 2007.

Spurgeon, Charles H. *Morning and Evening: Daily Readings,* Christian Classics Ethereal Library. Available from http://www.ccel.org/ccel/spurgeon/morneve.d1012am.html.

The Rule of the Society of Saint John the Evangelist. Lanham, Md: Rowman and Littlefield, Inc., 1997.

The Book of Common Prayer. New York: Church Publishing Incorporated, 1979.

Thomas à Kempis. *The Imitation of Christ.* Translated by Leo Sherley-Price. London: Penguin Books Ltd., 1952.

Thompson, Marjorie J. *Soul Feast: An Invitation to the Christian Spiritual Life.* Louisville, KY: Westminster John Knox, 1995.

Underhill, Evelyn. *Concerning the Inner Life.* New York: E.P. Dutton, 1926.

Vine, W.E.; Merrill Unger and William White. *Vine's Complete Expository Dictionary of Old and New Testament Words.* Nashville: Thomas Nelson, 1985.

Warfield, B.B. "The Emotional Life of Our Lord." Available at http://www.monergism.com/thethreshold/articles/onsite/emotionallife.html.

Webber, Robert. *Ancient Future Worship: Proclaiming and Enacting God's Narrative.* Grand Rapids: Baker Books, 2008.

_____. *The Divine Embrace.* Grand Rapids: Baker Books, 2006.

Wilhoit, James C. *Spiritual Formation as if the Church Mattered.* Grand Rapids: Baker Books, 2006.

Willard, Dallas. *Renovation of the Heart.* Colorado Springs: Nav Press, 2002.

_____. *The Spirit of the Disciplines: Understanding How God Changes Lives.* San Francisco: Harper One, 1990.

Wright, N.T. *The Early Christian Letters for Everyone.* Louisville: Westminster John Knox Press, 2011.

GRATITUDES

Gratitude is an offering precious in the sight of God, and it is one that the poorest of us can make and be not poorer but richer for having made it.

A.W. TOZER

We're truly rich in Christ, and as Tozer notes, even expressing our gratitude enriches our lives. What a generous God we serve. Here I want to express my heartfelt gratitude for my family, friends, and colleagues. *Thrive* is a community effort. I'm deeply grateful to my husband Jeff, and our children Cameron, Max, and Maddie, who've brought so much joy and meaning to my life, encouraging me along the way. I'm grateful to the leadership and members of Christ Church Plano for their support of this project, especially Rev. Daniel Adkinson and the Adult Discipleship Team. I'm grateful to Rosalie Mayo, Abby Celico, Melodie Thompson, Jane Schoen, and Shelley Frew for participating in the first test group of *Thrive* (offered as *Fidelity*). I'm grateful to many others who led small groups and worked through early versions of *Thrive*. I'm grateful to my friends and former colleagues in the Spiritual Formation Ministry at Dallas Theological Seminary, especially Barry Jones, Gail Seidel, Andy Seidel, Paul Pettit, Joye Baker, Brian Bittiker, Dipa Hart, and Terry Hebert. I learn so much from your faithful leadership, example, and scholarship. Finally, I'm grateful for the gifted team at Authenticity Book House, especially editor Trisha Mugo, artist A. J. Geiger, and founders Fran Geiger Joslin and Howard Joslin, for their joyful collaboration in publishing *Thrive*. Most of all I'm grateful to a God who truly desires our flourishing. We're blessed beyond measure in this life and in the life to come.

ABOUT THE AUTHOR

The Rev. Markene Meyer, an ordained minister in the Anglican Church in North America, enjoys helping people thrive in relationship with Christ and discover a more life-giving way.

A spiritual formation writer and spiritual director, Markene contributed to the Spiritual Formation curriculum at Dallas Theological Seminary, where she formerly served as Associate Director of Spiritual Formation.

Markene holds a doctor of ministry degree in spiritual formation. A lifelong Texan, she lives in the Lone Star State with her husband and three children.

Feel free to contact Markene.

meyer.markene@sbcglobal.net

www.facebook.com/thrive.markene.meyer

The Ministry of ABH

Authenticity Book House is a nonprofit publishing ministry that:

- Serves gifted Christian authors by removing publishing barriers.
- Equips non-English speaking pastors and teachers with biblical literature in their heart languages.
- Employs skilled believers in developing nations.

Serving Aspiring Authors

- Authors own all copyrights.
- ABH absorbs all costs for cover design, editing, formatting, proofreading, translating, and marketing of the author's first three books.
- ABH does not take any royalties on sales of the author's first three books.

Equipping Pastors Worldwide

- 20 percent of net royalties on all ABH books goes to support international pastors.
- ABH targets strategic language groups that lack biblical resources.

Empowering Believers

- ABH selects authors with confirmed Christlike character and ministry effectiveness.
- ABH employs translators and editors around the globe.

Please help us glorify Christ in editorial excellence. If you find a mistake in this book, please e-mail the error and the page number to quality@abhbooks.com.

50678796R00104

Made in the USA
Middletown, DE
03 November 2017